绿中国
GREEN CHINA

GREEN CHINA

HEATHER ANGEL

STACEY
INTERNATIONAL

Green China is based in part on an original idea by Martin Walters

Editor
Christopher Ind

Design
Graham Edwards

Stacey International
128 Kensington Church Street
London W8 4BH
Telephone: +44 (0)20 7221 7166
Fax: +44 (0)20 7792 9288
Email: info@stacey-international.co.uk
www.stacey-international.co.uk

ISBN: 978-1-905299-64-5

Half title page:
The lotus flower is regarded by Buddhists as a sacred symbol.

Title page:
A lone bamboo raft on the Lijiang is dwarfed by spiny bamboos and towering karst peaks.

This page:
A pair of Siberian tigers, in Heilongjiang, court in winter.

Contents

Introduction

For millennia, China was the land of invention and discovery, quantum leaps ahead of the rest of the world. Chinese scholars and artists also left a rich heritage of their vision of the natural world through their writings, poetry and paintings. Now after centuries of environmental mayhem with famines, wars and floods, China has a stable regime and is emerging as a world power. Home to 22 per cent of the world's population, hardly a day passes without China hitting the headline news in the West – be it a panda story, the worst weather in southern China for half a century, or a problem with pollution levels.

All statistics quoted in connection with China are awesome. In Beijing, workers no longer ride their bicycles ten abreast; many now opt to drive to work. But with a staggering 1,000 new cars appearing in the capital each day, commuting by car can be tedious; so some ingenious commuters have found using a combination of car, underground transit and bike can reduce their commuting time dramatically. These vast numbers of cars are exacerbating the aerial pollution problem from factories – especially from power and steel plants. In August 2007 one million private cars were taken off the Beijing roads each day for four days (all odd numbers one day and all even ones the next) in an attempt to reduce the pollution level.

China, of course, covers a vast area, but huge tracts – notably mountains and expansive deserts – are unsuitable for either agriculture or habitation. With 1.3 billion people to feed and house, it is a tricky equation balancing environmental protection with the aspirations of the burgeoning population.

Since the mid-1990s, China has seen unprecedented economic development and expansion. The dramatic acceleration in the pace of social development has been exceptional. In China, much of it has been at a great cost to the environment, which is becoming degraded or polluted. At the beginning of 2007, China's environment watchdog announced that the country had failed to reach its pollution control goals, because the economy grew faster than expected in 2006.

As people's lives have improved, their disposable income has risen (by 9.6 per cent in urban locations and 6.2 per cent in rural areas) and the desire to travel further afield – both in China and overseas – has increased. Recently, there has been a massive building of expressways and airports giving speedier access to previously remote locations. At the same time, a plethora of new hotels have been built to accommodate rising tourist levels. Once a highway or a local airport has been built adjacent to a beautiful reserve, developers move in and the floodgates open for mass tourism. For example, since the beautiful mountain Nine Village Valley known as Jiuzhaigou began to charge visitors in 1984, the demand has become so great that a limit has now been set to a maximum of 28,000 tourists a day to this Sichuan hotspot.

Many scientists, NGOs and governmental organisations are well aware of what China has to lose if steps are not taken to redress the balance of the impact on the natural environment. If nothing is done, quite simply a green China will soon be history. Everyone, from individuals to the Chinese Government, is talking about environmental protection. Indeed, steps are being taken to expand the alternative energy programme, with solar panels springing up like mushrooms, not just in cities, but also in remote areas as well. Huge wind power parks are appearing both inland and on the coast.

Even though there has been a rapid growth in the declaration of protected areas at every level, from local nature reserves, NNRs, National Parks to WHS and MAB reserves, there is no room for complacency. Declaration of a reserve on paper is only a first step, which has to be followed through with a good management structure and adequate staff training in order to enforce the regulations. Illegal fishing and hunting will cease only if alternative means of earning a living can be found.

Opposite:
A natural window frames the landform, known as Earth Forest, at Yuanmou, Yunnan.

As species after species drop to highly critical levels, a dedicated band of conservationists, biologists and naturalists work tirelessly to rescue them. The giant panda, as the country's national treasure, gets the most publicity; but there are, in fact, many rarer animals. Examples of species to have been brought back from the brink of extinction include Eld's deer, the Chinese alligator and the crested ibis.

The Chinese Government is aiming to reduce the major pollutants by ten per cent during the five-year period 2006-10. At the same time, it aims to reduce energy consumption by 20 per cent. An allocation of 1.4 trillion yuan (US$154bn) has been set aside for protecting the environment by improving water quality, reducing soil erosion as well as cutting pollution in the air and on land. However, SEPA has admitted that the scheme aimed to curb pollution by the withdrawal of loans has not met their projected targets. In July 2007, the green credit policy was launched whereby SEPA would pass on the names of major polluting companies to the central bank. These companies would then not be eligible for future loans.

Education is playing a key role in getting people to understand the natural world is not inexhaustible and therefore cannot be exploited relentlessly. Already there are signs of a growing environmental awareness with recycling depots and bins now much in evidence. In 2006, an enterprising young person's environmental group known as Green Eyes was established. Where they find people exploiting the environment, they shoot videos to provide evidence of pollution or of endangered animals for sale in markets. Working with the police they have had many positive results with criminal prosecutions.

Farming communities, who have been dependent on the land for generations, understand about sustainability. Native plants of commercial value were collected selectively or on rotation, which allowed time for the plants to regenerate. Problems arise when these plants become threatened by mass collection. Knowledge about how medicinal plants grow and reproduce themselves will help to conserve them. For

Below:
This map shows the provinces and semi-autonomous regions that make up modern-day China.

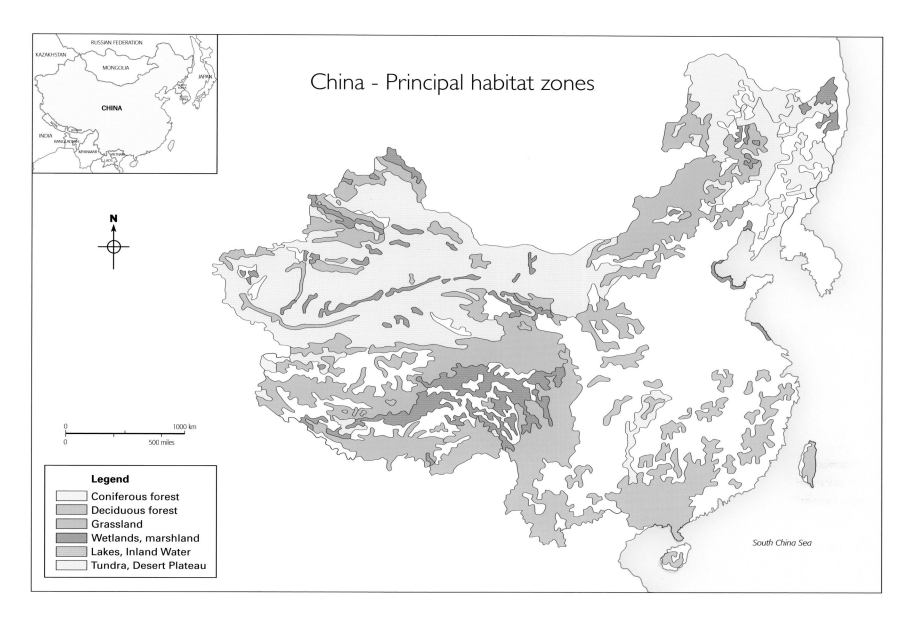

China - Principal habitat zones

Legend
- Coniferous forest
- Deciduous forest
- Grassland
- Wetlands, marshland
- Lakes, Inland Water
- Tundra, Desert Plateau

South China Sea

Above:
This map indicates the major habitat zones of China. While their extent is approximate, the map serves to highlight the variety of habitats, often intermingled. White areas indicate cultivated land and urban areas.

instance, snow lotus with a long taproot is killed once this is uprooted or broken, whereas plants that have an underground rhizome system, like the katuka, survive if only part of the rhizome is left behind.

Green China is a celebration of China's wilder areas – of forests and wetlands, coastlines and caves as well as mountains and deserts. Waiting to be fully discovered and appreciated are stunning landscapes – some quite unique, exquisite wildflowers, a galaxy of birds and a rich assortment of mammals. As eco-tourism begins to expand in China, more overseas visitors will get a chance to explore beyond the tourist icons such as the Summer Palace, the Great Wall or the Terracotta Warriors in Xi'an. Many will be surprised at the wealth of riches. A century or more ago, plant hunters in China appreciated the rich species diversity within many parts of Yunnan and Sichuan, though the concepts of biodiversity and hotspots were yet to be recognised. Today we know China to be one of the world's most biologically diverse countries.

I do believe that China has the will and determination to implement the Green Revolution for a brighter future for all China and the enjoyment of overseas visitors. China is expected to replace France as the world's top tourist destination by 2014 – if not sooner. Hopefully by then the city air will be cleaner, the water quality improved, landscapes will be protected and ecosystems preserved, and this book will not serve as a record of China's glorious past.

Author's acknowledgements

Many people helped in the production of this book. I am especially indebted to Martin Walters and Donna Xiao for providing, early on, useful contacts in China who gave me advice about where to find certain species. The following people advised me on specific topics or sites: Gerard Burgermeister based in Jinghong, advised about Xishuangbanna and the Mekong area in general. He also runs a delightful B&B in a lush tropical garden with his wife Lynn. Superb private villas are built from recycled hardwood overlooking the Mekong River (www.yourantai.com). Dr Aili Kang, West China Project, WCS China for advice about the Gansu Endangered Wildlife Breeding Centre; Eve Li, Siberian Tiger Project, WCS China on the Siberian tiger status; Dr Sun Song on Shandong coastlines and mariculture; He Fen-Qi on pheasants; Huang Huahai on Yunnan flora and Steve Hootman on rhododendrons.

Many others helped to arrange my tailor-made itineraries with transport and guides. Most especially I thank: Jia Min of China Bird Tours (www.birdschina.com); Henry Wang, Xanadu Tour (www.xanadutour.com); Pan Shijun (www.guilinphototours.com); Vicky Apel who arranged my trip to Wild Elephant Valley (www.biodiversitycentre.com) and offers tailor-made trekking tours through minority villages, tea plantations and forests with English-speaking guides; Sophie Song and Mary Chen for travel arrangements in and out of Shanghai.

Other organisations I travelled with include: China Span (www.chinaspan.com); Joe Van Os Photo Safaris (www.photosafaris.com); Naturetrek (www.naturetrek.co.uk) and Sunbird (www.sunbirdtours.co.uk).

I am greatly indebted to all my guides and drivers who helped me achieve my goals – sometimes against all odds. Professor Shi Haitao of Hainan Normal University was quite brilliant at fixing difficult objectives at very short notice and I owe him a great debt. Zhang Hai very kindly showed me around Datian Nature Reserve at a weekend and explained the work involved in the successful rearing of the endangered Eld's deer. Mr Yuan Xue Shun, Director of the Weihai Swan Protection Association, gave up a whole day to tell me about Rongcheng Swan Nature Reserve and take me to the most photogenic sites. I also thank Dr Zhang Hemin, Director of the China Conservation and Research Center for the Giant Panda, and his staff for assistance with photography at Wolong. Mr Xu Zenian, Manager of the Gansu Endangered Wildlife Breeding Centre, very kindly provided access for photography.

It would have been impossible for me to complete the copy in such a short space of time, without the extensive research done from my office by Lucy Simpson who struggled with aging fax machines in remote parts of China where there were no internet connections. She also typed and proofread most of the copy, with help from Kate Carter. We managed to persuade my old personal assistant, Valerie West, to come out of retirement to produce the index. Justin Harrison and Ed Pugh assisted me with the digital side. Thanks to you all for a great team effort.

Special thanks go to my husband, Martin Angel, who has – as always – encouraged me throughout and came with me on his first China trip searching for alpines in Yunnan. Our son, Giles, also a photographer, accompanied me on part of two trips – which meant I had a wider range of equipment to use.

Finally, my thanks to the team at Stacey International, for taking this project on board with great enthusiasm and for making it their flagship book of the year.

Opposite:
Bamboo leaves in Anhui are backlit by the sun.

Chinese Dynasties

Xia Dynasty (c. 2000- c. 1500 BC)

Shang Dynasty (ca. 1700-ca. 1000 BC)

Zhou Dynasty (1027-256 BC)
    Western Zhou Dynasty (c. Eleventhy century-771 BC)
    Eastern Zhou Dynasty (c. 770-256 BC)
                - Spring and Autumn Period (770-476 BC)
                - Warring States (475-221 BC)

Qin Dynasty (221-206 BC)

Han Dynasty (206 BC-AD 220)
    Western Han Dynasty (206 BC-AD 25)
    Eastern Han Dynasty (25-220)

Three Kingdoms (220-280)
    Wei (220-265)
    Shu Han (221-263)
    Wu (222-280)

Jin Dynasty (265-420)
    Western Jin Dynasty (265-316)
    Eastern Jin Dynasty (317-420)

Southern and Northern Dynasties (420-589)
    Southern Dynasties (420-589)
    Northern Dynasties (368-581)
                - Sui Dynasty (581-618)
                - Tang Dynasty (618-907)

Five Dynasties (907-960)

Song Dynasty (960-1279)
    Northern Song Dynasty (960-1127)
    Southern Song Dynasty (1127-1279)

Liao Dynasty (916-1125)

Western Xia (1038-1227)

Jin Dynasty (1115-1234)

Yuan Dynasty (1271-1368)

Ming Dynasty (1368-1644)

Qing Dynasty (1644-1911)

Abbreviations

AR – Autonomous Region

BR – UNESCO Biosphere Reserve

MAB – UNESCO Man and Biosphere Programme

NG – National Geopark

NGO – Non-Governmental Organisation

NNR – National Nature Reserve

NP – **National Park**

NR – Nature Reserve

NRP – National Rainforest Park

SAR – Special Administrative Region

SEPA – State Environmental Protection Agency

TCM – Traditional Chinese Medicine

UNESCO – United Nations Educational, Scientific and Cultural Organisation

WHS – UNESCO World Heritage Site

WCS – Wildlife Conservation Society

WWF – World Wide Fund for Nature

1

People and Wildlife

China has the richest assortment of terrestrial ecosystems anywhere in the world. The diverse array of flora and fauna includes Eurasian species spreading from the north, tropical species invading from the south as well as a large number of endemic species unique to China. One example of the interactions between people and wildlife in China is the ancient custom of training cormorants to fish, which was first recorded in 221 BC.

Fishermen on the Lijiang still use the traditional method of fishing from bamboo rafts using lights to attract the fish and cormorants to catch them.

Historical connections

In terms of conservation stakes, China may not yet be so advanced as many Western countries, but we should not forget that this, the world's oldest civilisation, was way ahead – by hundreds and sometimes thousands of years – in many discoveries and inventions. It is well known that the Chinese invented gunpowder, fireworks and the wheel; less well known are the discoveries that relate to the natural world. Snowflakes were found to be hexagonal (second century BC), waterpower was harnessed (first century AD) and biological pest control implemented (third century AD).

When kites were invented in China some 2,400 years ago, they were made of wood and bamboo; later they were constructed from silk or paper. Around 444 BC, a wooden kite shaped as an eagle was used by the Chu Kingdom to spy on the Song Kingdom. It was not until AD 784 when cloth and paper kites were designed to carry lighted candles, that they caught the imagination of the people. Flown at night, the lights twinkled and swayed as the kite moved in the breeze. Then elaborate designs and colours began to be painted on the paper so they glowed from the inner lights. The cost of these kites prohibited their use by all except the nobility and the gentry. However, after the kites got carried in strong winds, crashed to the ground and set fire to straw and wood, they were banned. Flying paper or silk kites remains a popular pastime, so it is commonplace to see dragons as well as birds, butterflies, dragonflies and fish snaking through the skies above public parks and even above Shanghai's famous Bund.

The first zoo to be established was in China in 1000 BC by King Wen Wang. He called his Imperial Zoo Ling-Yu or the 'Garden of Intelligence' where the animals in his collection could be studied and also provide pleasure. Being in possession of a giant panda (*Ailuropoda melanoleuca*) was considered to be a great status symbol and so these animals were often to be found amongst the Emperor's menagerie within the Palace Gardens in Xi'an. Indeed, wildlife must have been sufficiently valued during the life of Qin Shi Huang (221-206 BC), the first Emperor of China, for birds to be

Above:
A silk butterfly kite rides above Beijing.

Left:
The tiger – one of Tibet's four mythical creatures – is painted on the wall of a Tibetan house at Suzheng Village, Jiuzhaigou, Sichuan.

Opposite above:
One of nine large dragons frolics in the clouds in a mural on each side of the Nine Dragon Wall in Beihai Park, Beijing, which was built in 1756 during the Qing Dynasty.

Opposite below:
The wingless female glow-worm, photographed from beneath, produces a luminous glow at night from her abdomen, to attract a mate.

included in a recently discovered pit sited between the famous terracotta warriors and the Emperor's tomb mound. Here, together with terracotta acrobats, are whole flocks of bronze cranes as well as bronze swans placed on artificial lakes within buried gardens.

Bioluminescence, or living light, has for long intrigued the Chinese, who called it 'yin fire'. By AD 10, natural luminescence was used to make phosphorescent paintings. A Chinese legend tells how the family of a student called Che Yin were so poor they could not afford to buy any oil to provide a lamp for him to study at night. So, each evening he would go out to collect enough female glow-worms (*Lampyris noctiluca*) to provide light for him to read.

Animal and plant symbolism

Symbols of the natural world – both real and mythical – have a long history in China and still abound today as wall paintings, on buildings, and on ornamental windows or as mosaics in classical gardens.

Tibetan traditions have close links to nature, with four mythical creatures – the dragon, tiger, snow-lion and garuda that represent the four elements: water, wind or air, earth and fire. The dragon (water) is associated with clouds and thunder and represents power. The tiger (wind), inspired by the natural animal, conveys courage. The youthful energy of the snow-lion (earth) is associated with fearfulness, while the garuda (fire) is a huge bird, which symbolises wisdom, and power over evil spirits.

The dragon was originally the symbol of the Emperor of China – indeed the imperial throne was known as the Dragon Throne. Nowadays, the dragon is no longer the national emblem of China, although Hong Kong uses a fiery coloured dragon to promote the brand name of their city overseas. Dragons nonetheless still abound in China; at the time of the Chinese New Year, people flock to see the dragon boat racing and vibrant dragon dancing where a huge dragon snakes along supported by poles carried by several people.

Over many centuries, the dragon has gradually changed from being a ferocious looking beast to becoming a gentler tame one. The colour was also significant: yellow were the most revered, so the emperor's gowns were decorated with yellow dragons. During the late Qing Dynasty, when the dragon appeared on the national flag, no commoner could be seen wearing a dragon symbol, because it was considered to be a capital offence.

It is not certain what animal inspired the original dragon. Some say it was a giant crocodile, which ties in with the mythical belief of the dragon's dominance over water. The dragon is included amongst the twelve animals of the Chinese zodiac, which is a 12-year period based on the lunar cycle used for dating the years. More babies are born in a dragon year than in any other zodiac animal year.

Plants, too, have symbolic connotations. The lotus (*Nelumbo nucifera*) is a plant with an exquisitely beautiful flower, which unlike the floating water lily, rises above the surface to bloom. Because the lotus symbolises purity and perfection, Buddhists all over the world recognise it as the holy seat of Buddha. Once grown in special lotus pots within courtyards, today most Chinese public gardens still have an ornamental lotus pond or lake.

The chrysanthemum, a popular flower of Confucian scholars, became known as one of the 'Four Gentlemen of Flowers' together with the bamboo, orchid and plum flower. It symbolises *yang* energy and if placed in the home is thought to bring good luck. Buddhists also offer this flower at the altar. Chrysanthemums have been extensively cultivated in China to produce outsized simple blooms, sporting an amazing array of colours as well as petal shapes. They may even be trained into long cascades or carefully manipulated into impressive circular displays with all the heads equidistantly spaced supported on a wire or bamboo framework. Special chrysanthemum displays are staged up and down the country within China's Golden Week during the first week of October.

Orchids, cultivated in China for at least 2,500 years, often feature in paintings, poetry and literature. *Cymbidium* species were amongst the earliest orchids to be grown in China where they are so esteemed it is considered a great honour to be given one of these fragrant blooms; particularly since they convey friendship.

Above:
Centuries of breeding chrysanthemums have produced many novel flower shapes, such as this spider chrysanthemum on display at a flower show in the Botanical Garden, Urumqi.

Below left:
Grown in Imperial Palace gardens during the Sui and Tang Dynasties, the peony was known as the 'King of Flowers' and regarded as a symbol of nobility. Tree peonies are still popular plants in parks and gardens today.

Opposite:
A dawn sun catches the sacred lotus bud before its warming rays persuade it to unfurl.

PÈRE ARMAND DAVID

Père Armand David (1826-1900) was a French missionary with a great passion for the natural world. Initially, he managed to combine his career as a priest with extensive natural science studies. His first posting was to a school in Italy, where he taught science for ten years before getting his dream destination – China – in 1863.

Whilst there, he was instructed to collect specimens for the Musée d'Histoire Naturelle in Paris. The extent of his collections – all meticulously preserved and documented – proved to be of such value to specialists at the Paris Museum, it was eventually decided Père David could relinquish his teaching duties so he could devote all his time to his collections. Their scope was further extended when the Jardin des Plantes commissioned him to collect plant material on their behalf.

Quite a few new species of plants and animals were eventually named after Père David, but his name is inextricably linked with two Chinese mammals. He was the first Westerner to set eyes on a giant panda – albeit a skin in a Sichuan hunter's hut. As soon as he saw the black and white pelt, he realised it was a species new to science. David requested hunters to capture an intact specimen, but he left China without ever seeing a living giant panda.

He played a key part in saving an unusual deer from the brink of extinction. Originally called *sibuxiang* meaning 'unlike any of the four' because the deer appeared as a mixture of four different animals – a deer's antlers, a camel's neck, a cow's broad hoofs and a donkey's tail. Now known in China as *milu*, they lived in marshlands within the Yangtze River basin, where they readily wade or swim through water. Male *milu* grow two sets of antlers in a year, which are unusual in having their points directed backwards.

Loss of wetland habitat and over-hunting caused the *milu* population to plummet in the nineteenth century. Fortunately, the Emperor of China had gathered a large herd of *milu* within the Nanyuan Imperial Hunting Park or Nan Haizi, on the outskirts of Peking (Beijing), before they became extinct in the wild in the early part of the twentieth century.

Late in the autumn of 1865, Père David approached the Imperial Park on a donkey and rode up a hill to get a clear view over the wall. He was amazed to see such strange looking deer, so he stayed in the area observing them from outside the Park until the following spring.

During this time, he hatched a plot whereby in exchange for coins placed inside a drainpipe, running beneath the wall, a park guard would send a *milu* skull and some skin back down the pipe. After telling the French Embassy of his discovery, two live deer were obtained which enabled David to send his description of this new species to Paris. This caused quite a stir because it turned out to be a new sub-genus of deer. In recognition of David's work, it became known as Père David's deer (*Elaphurus davidianus*).

Ironically, it was from amongst the *milu* assembled purely for sport that the species was saved from extinction. After Père David alerted the outside world of the deer's existence, the French Ambassador persuaded the Emperor to donate deer to European zoos. In 1895 catastrophic flooding broke the wall of the Imperial Park releasing the deer. Hunted for food, they gradually became eliminated.

In 1898 the eleventh Duke of Bedford rescued the last remaining eighteen deer from Europe, bringing them to his wild animal park at Woburn Abbey in Bedfordshire. After five years the herd had increased to 37 animals; by the First World War there were 88, reaching 255 by the onset of the Second World War.

It was then decided to evacuate some of the Père David's deer to North America and Europe. In 1985 20 deer were reintroduced to China in the Imperial Park (now known as Beijing Milu Park).

During his multiple trips to China, over an eleven-year period, Père David collected no less than 807 species of birds, 65 of which had not been described before, 200 species of mammals (63 new to science). In addition to reptiles, amphibians, fish and insects, he also collected many new plants, including 52 new species of rhododendrons.

Among the other species named after Père David are the Chinese giant salamander (*Andrias davidianus*); the pocket handkerchief or dove tree (*Davidia involucrata*) which produces flowers that have a pair of white dove-like bracts; the butterfly bush (*Buddleia davidii*); a lily (*Lilium davidii*) and Père David's maple (*Acer davidii*). Père David's biological knowledge combined with his inquisitive mind introduced a remarkable range of Chinese flora and fauna to the Western world.

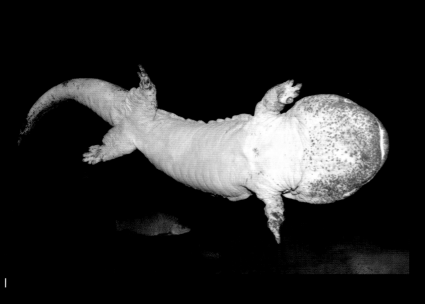

1

2

5

7

3

Utilising nature

One of the most important discoveries was the origin of silk. Sericulture or silk production was thought to have originated in China some 4,000 years ago, but recent finds in sites along the lower Yangtze River have unearthed a small 6,000-7,000 year-old cup bearing a silkworm design, as well as spinning tools and silk thread. The silkworm moth (*Bombyx mori*) is native to China. After mating, the female moth is very productive and lays 500 tiny eggs over 4-5 days before she dies. One ounce of eggs produces 30,000 larvae (the silkworms), which eat a ton of white mulberry (*Morus alba*) leaves. The mature larva spins a cocoon formed from a single 600-900 metre-long silk thread, changing inside the cocoon into a pupa or chrysalis after the final moult. The silk can be unravelled only after plunging the cocoon into boiling water to loosen the silken filament. Five to seven filaments are combined to produce the silk thread and it takes nearly 6,000 cocoons to produce one kilo of silk. According to Chinese legend, the silk was first discovered by Empress Hsi Ling Shi, the wife of Emperor Huang-ti, whilst she was drinking tea beneath a mulberry tree when a cocoon dropped into her cup and the silken thread began to unfurl.

Starting from Xi'an, China's ancient capital, merchant caravans carried the precious silk fabrics across deserts and through mountain passes to the Mediterranean along what later became known as the Silk Road. China managed to keep the origin of silk production a closely guarded secret for thousands of years until the third century AD. Several people came up with some wild guesses. One of these was Pliny in his *Natural History* where he wrote in 70 BC that 'silk was obtained by removing down from leaves'.

The Chinese were making paper in the second century BC, 1,300 years before it was manufactured in the West. Today, handmade paper is a dying art as young people are attracted to busy cities for more lucrative jobs and more exciting leisure activities than a rural community can offer. Even so, there are still a few places along the Silk Road and in southern Yunnan where it is possible to see elderly people producing handmade paper. Many different plants can be used for papermaking, but the most popular one is the bark of one-year-old white mulberry. This is stripped from the branches and softened in water before being boiled in a large vessel. Once cooled, the softened bark is repeatedly pummelled with a wooden mallet on a stone slab before

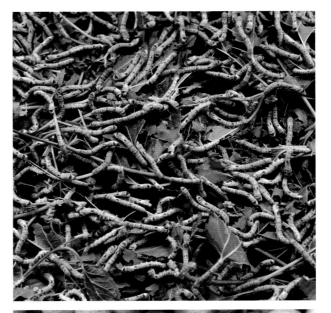

Preceding pages:
Roses are harvested early in the early morning for rose wine (*Mei gui*) in a Hotan small holding.

Top:
Silkworms are reared in large shallow trays on white mulberry leaves, which are changed daily.

Above:
Before silk can be harvested from the cocoons, they are placed in boiling water to kill the pupae and help unravel the silk thread.

Left:
Silk from silkworm cocoons is unravelled in a heated copper pan in Hotan on the Silk Road.

the bark purée is mixed with a volume of water, which varies according to the thickness of paper required. The mix is then poured onto a muslin sheet stretched taut onto a wooden frame, which is stacked vertically so the surplus water drains away. On a hot sunny day, it is not long before the dry paper can be peeled away from the frame.

Many Chinese wines are produced today from grapes, but with a 4,000-year-old history of wine making, many other plants were used to make wine – notably rice, wheat and sorghum. A sweet dessert wine known as *Mei gui*, is made from rose petals. Mounds of deep pink rose petals appear beside the streets of Hotan on the southern Silk Route between 10 May and 10 June, when the roses are picked. The petals have to be plucked free from the stamens otherwise the wine would have a bitter taste.

Attitudes to wildlife

Interactions between people and wildlife in China go back several millennia. Animal bones (ox shoulder blades) and turtle shells with Chinese characters incised in them have been found dating back to the late Shang Dynasty (1200-1050 BC), not from an archaeological dig, but by an observant patient. When he fell ill in 1899, he was prescribed *longgu* or dragon bones. Later he realised they were tortoise shells and saw they bore inscriptions, so he kept them and showed them to a scholar. It was later discovered they came from the site of the remains of the Shang Dynasty capital in Henan.

The traditional attitude of people to wildlife in China is very different from the Western philosophy. China's long history of wars, catastrophic floods and famines has played a major role in Chinese attitudes to nature. On the one hand, it is generally regarded as subservient to human welfare and economic development and can justifiably be exploited. On the other, nature is admired; an inspiration for Chinese art and influence in garden design.

For many traditional Chinese people, a wild species is worth conserving only if it can be shown to be useful to people, as food, medicine, or because it is beautiful, so the concept of preserving nature simply for its own sake is somewhat alien to many people.

Above:
The first stage in making handmade paper from inner mulberry bark is to boil the strips of bark in a large wok, here in Hotan.

Above:
Rose petals plucked from freshly picked roses, ready for collection by the rose wine factory in Hotan.

Right:
Shallow trays stacked up for drying handmade paper in the sun in southern Yunnan.

PLANT HUNTERS

Many of the magnolias, camellias, rhododendrons, paeonies, lilies and primulas that we enjoy in temperate gardens today originate from China. We owe a great debt to a handful of dedicated plant hunters – mostly from Europe – who collected so many botanical riches, chiefly from Yunnan, Sichuan and Tibet AR and introduced them to Western horticulture in the nineteenth and twentieth centuries, suffering hardships and in some cases, risking their lives in the process.

Fortune, Robert (1812-80)
Born in Scotland, Fortune made his first trip to China in 1843 at the bequest of the Royal Horticultural Society based in Chiswick, London. After three years plant-hunting he returned with new azalea, rhododendron and forsythia species. From Chinese gardens he introduced a rampant climbing hybrid rose *Rosa x fortuniana*, with scented double flowers, which thrives in a warm climate. Other plants named in his honour include *Hosta fortunei*, *Mahonia fortunei* and *Rhododendron fortunei*. In 1848 he returned to China to collect tea (*Camellia sinensis*) seeds and plants; Fortune sent these to India and became the founder of the India Tea industry.

Delavay, Père Jean Marie (1838-95)
Père Delavay first arrived in China as a French missionary in 1867, four years after Père David (see p8). Working in the Yunnan mountains, Delavay collected 1,500 species new to Western botanists and brought back the seeds of many rhododendrons. He discovered the silver fir *Abies delavayi* in 1984, *Paeonia delavayi* and the two-metre-high *Thalictrum delavayi* with delicate lilac flowers bearing cream stamens; all are named after him.

Forrest, George (1873-1932)
This Scottish plant collector made seven trips to China between 1904-1932, collecting many *primulas* as well as rhododendrons – including *Rhododendron giganteum* and *R. sinogrande* from Yunnan and Tibet – for Edinburgh Botanic Garden. He introduced many plants first discovered by Père Delavay. A snakebark maple known as Forrest's maple (*Acer forrestii*) and the fir *Abies forrestii* are both named after Forrest.

Wilson, E.H 'Chinese' (1876-1930)
One of the most famous of all the plant hunters, Wilson made several trips to China from 1899-1911 discovering over 3,000 species. Whilst working at Kew, the Director put forward his name to the Veitch Nursery who wanted someone to collect *Davidia involucrata*. In 1899, Wilson not only found the handkerchief tree, but also 400 new plants. His next goal was the exquisite alpine yellow poppy (*Meconopsis integrifolia*) and he returned from Sichuan with this plus rhododendrons, primulas, roses and the regal lily (*Lilium regale*). From 1906, the Arnold Arboretum in Boston sponsored his next two expeditions. When Wilson returned to the Min Valley in 1910 to collect more regal lily bulbs, he nearly lost a leg when an avalanche of boulders crushed it as he was carried in a sedan chair. The tripod he used for his whole plate Sanderson camera was used to set his broken leg, but thereafter Wilson walked with what he referred to as his 'lily limp'. In recognition of his contributions to Chinese introductions, Americans coined the nickname 'Chinese' Wilson.

Farrer, Reginald (1880-1920)
After studying at Oxford, where he helped to make the rock garden at St John's College, Farrer left in 1902 on his first expedition to Asia, visiting China, Korea and Japan. He had strong views on rock garden design and wrote many books on alpines suitable for rock gardens. He returned to China in 1914 with William Purdom to explore and collect from Gansu. As well as collecting specimens and seeds, Farrer produced watercolours of many plants – often in difficult field conditions. Amongst the plants named after him are *Viburnum farreri*, *Gentiana farreri* and *Primula farreri*. Farrer died on his own in Burma at the premature age of forty.

Rock, Joseph (1884-1962)
An American, of Austrian birth, Joseph Rock's first trip to China (sponsored by the National Geographic Society and the Smithsonian Institution) was many years after other collectors had worked in China. Nonetheless, the three years spent in Yunnan from 1922-1924 produced almost 80,000 specimens for the Smithsonian's herbarium. In addition to his field notes, Rock took photographs of the plants and their habitat. Later, he worked further north up to the Min Shan range and the upper reaches of the Yellow River (Huang He). He collected the birch *Betula albo-sinensis* with the attractive peeling reddish bark.

Kingdom Ward, Frank (1885-1958)
Son of a Professor of Botany, Kingdom-Ward gained his Natural Sciences Tripos at Cambridge, before setting off in 1907 to teach at a school in Shanghai. He aspired to be a plant hunter and his first chance came when he was invited to collect plants in Yunnan by a Liverpool nursery, who had lost their plant collector – George Forrest – to Caerhays Castle in Cornwall. In 1913, Kingdom-Ward collected in Yunnan and Tibet and after serving in the First World War, he returned to China several times, discovering the exquisite yellow giant cowslip *Primula florindae*, which naturally thrives beside streams and in wet meadows, now much favoured for planting in bog gardens. He also brought back the fabulous Himalayan blue poppy (*Meconopsis betonicifolia*).

Some of the Chinese plants had to be carefully nurtured to survive in Britain or North America; in fact Professor Sargeant, Director of Arnold Aboretum, sent some of Wilson's plants, which were too tender for the warm Boston climate, back to Scotland, where they can be seen at Dawyck Arboretum. On the other hand, the butterfly bush has escaped from many a suburban garden to become a weed along railway lines and on waste ground.

Opposite:
1. *Paeonia rockii* is a striking tree peony introduced to the West from south-west Gansu by Joseph Rock.

2. Seeds of Dawson's magnolia (*Magnolia dawsoniana*) were collected by E.H. Wilson in Sichuan in 1908.

3. George Forrest collected the Chinese pagoda primrose (*Primula vialii*) in Yunnan in 1906.

4. In 1903 E.H. Wilson travelled 600 miles for *Meconopsis punicea*, with petals like crushed tissue paper.

5. The shrub *Pieris formosa* var *forrestii*, with attractive new red growth was introduced by Forrest in 1903.

6. Chusan palm (*Trachycarpus fortunei*) in flower; introduced by Robert Fortune in 1849.

7. *Nomocharis aperta* (*N. forrestii*) growing in alpine grassland near Zhongdian, Yunnan.

8. The regal lily bulbs collected by E.H. 'Chinese' Wilson in 1910 now grace many an English garden.

1

2

3

4

5

6

7

8

Urban living dominates much of China, especially in the east coast strip, but in rural areas many people continue to live their lives much closer to nature. As always, a balance has to be struck between providing better living standards for the many millions of urban dwellers, improving transport and generating power, and a more caring and gentler attitude towards nature. With China's rapid economic growth in recent years, the problems of pollution and habitat destruction are arguably more extreme here. Nonetheless, the worldwide problems of desertification, air and water pollution, flooding and soil infertility are global and these are warning signs that natural resources are being overexploited. In the years ahead, China will have to meet these challenges and come up with workable solutions.

Now the effects of global warming are bringing 'green' issues to the forefront of debate and political decision-making as never before. It is encouraging that the 2007 People's Congress placed conservation firmly on the agenda in the latest five-year plan.

Both Chinese food and traditional Chinese medicine (TCM) are closely connected with the natural world. TCM has a history of some 3,000 years when a pharmacopoeia of herbal combinations found to be effective remedies evolved gradually through centuries of trial and error, largely passed down through generations by word of mouth. Such activities inevitably raise ethical queries, especially when animal parts are used in traditional medicine, but many recent pressures have been caused by commercialisation of what was once a less intrusive local tradition. The Wildlife Conservation Society (WCS) has initiated a public awareness campaign on the use of TCM, which often use endangered species like the tiger as their main ingredients; while the World Wide Fund for Nature (WWF) have instigated a TCM Program which involves promoting the way recently discovered herbs can be used as substitutes for animal parts.

The eating of rare animal species is anathema to Westerners but acceptable practice in China, which consumes more wildlife than any other country. The problem is exacerbated with new-found wealth generating more up-market banquets featuring exotic species. Pangolins have become more popular since the crackdown in the trade of endangered species in the Indo-Pacific region. Endangered species are often ordered in restaurants by using a code.

For centuries, birds, and also crickets, have been kept in cages to enjoy their entertaining sounds and songs. Even today, an early morning or afternoon stroll in a public park will find elderly men, each sitting beside their bamboo cage housing a songbird, such as a Pekin robin (*Leiothrix lutea*), often competing with each other for the best voices, and with no hint of sympathy for their imprisoned charges. Fish are kept as symbols of prosperity and admired for their beauty. Colourful varieties of Koi carp are often kept in ornamental ponds, in formal gardens and zoos as well as in hotel lobbies.

China's ethnic minorities

China has a diverse ethnic culture with 56 separate ethnic groups being recognised; the Hani with around 92 per cent is by far the largest. The minority groups have centuries of environmental knowledge – not least which native plants can be eaten or used for medicine. Now, multinational companies and their researchers are beginning to tap this native knowledge bank in the search for new drugs and treatments.

The Miao use traditional wooden boats and wooden irrigation systems. The Yi worship nature spirits – trees, rocks, water, sky, earth, wind and forests – as well as their ancestors, and some regard the mythical Chinese dragons as their protectors.

Above:
Colourful ornamental goldfish and Koi carp are always a popular feature within ponds and lakes in large Chinese public parks and gardens.

Left:
Many minorities wear their traditional dress for festive occasions. This rear view of a Miao girl from Guizhou in festive dress, shows off the pretty head-dress and the ornate back panel worn for the Miao lusheng dance.

Below:
Dwarf banana or golden lotus (*Musella lasiocarpa*), endemic to south-west Yunnan mountains, is a sacred flower of local Buddhism.

Opposite above:
A Dai house is built on two levels: the lower open one is used for feeding livestock, with the family living accommodation on the upper floor. Here, coconut palms in south subtropical Yunnan frame the vegetable garden.

Opposite below:
A Dai girl wears a skirt with a peacock feather design as she collects water from a well in southern Yunnan.

The Dong are perhaps best known for their architecture, notably their unique covered ('wind and rain') bridges. The Yao build rectangular houses using wood and bamboo, as do the Dai and Hani, making good use of often sustainable and fully biodegradable raw materials.

The Dai are mainly Buddhist and live mostly close to the Lancang (Mekong) River in the south of Yunnan. They regard the peacock as a very special bird, which symbolises happiness, good fortune, beauty and kindness. Indeed, the elaborate plumage and displays of this magnificent bird have inspired a traditional peacock dance. Performers wear costumes that mimic the peacock plumage – especially the eyespots in the tail feathers – using bird-like movements; they combine jerky gestures with graceful sweeps.

Many ethnic groups, including the Hani, wear dark blue clothing dyed using vegetable indigo (*landian yao*). In Guizhou, the leaves of Chinese rain bell (*Strobilanthes cusia*) are soaked in water inside wooden barrels where they ferment, a process which may take several days or weeks, depending on the temperature. After removing the leaves, lime is added and the mixture beaten. Once it has formed a crusty blue froth, the water is scooped out, leaving the indigo paste.

Conservation initiatives

Environmental protection and sustainability are phrases frequently heard in China today as people begin to appreciate they do not have an inexhaustible supply of natural resources. China's first nature reserve was established in 1956 and half a century later the number has increased to over 2,000 covering 15 per cent of the total

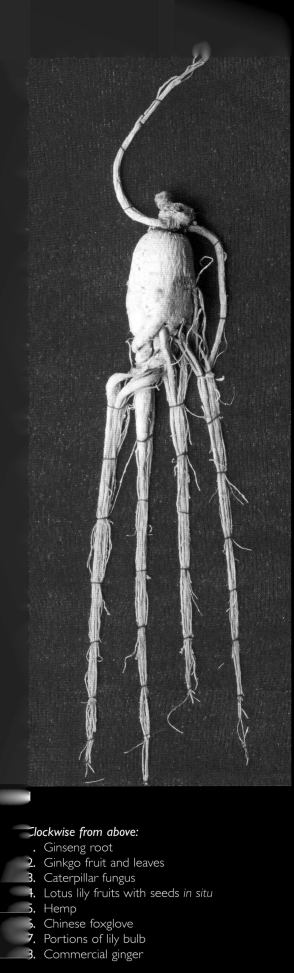

2

3

8

4

7

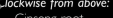

Clockwise from above:
1. Ginseng root
2. Ginkgo fruit and leaves
3. Caterpillar fungus
4. Lotus lily fruits with seeds *in situ*
5. Hemp
6. Chinese foxglove
7. Portions of lily bulb
8. Commercial ginger

MEDICINAL PLANTS

The first known Chinese herb book dates back to 2,700 BC and lists 365 medicinal plants. Since then, thousands of different plants have been used in traditional Chinese medicine (TMC), and several hundred are regularly used in herbal shops today. Recent scientific research has identified active components in some TCM plants. After testing, wormwood (*Artemisia annua*) was found to be effective against many strains of the malarial parasite, and the endemic cucumber-relative *Trichosanthes kirilowii* strongly active against HIV, the cause of AIDS.

The Chinese Medicinal Plants Authentication Centre (CMPAC) at the Royal Botanic Gardens, Kew, in London, provides an authentication service for the increasing range of Chinese herbs currently available on the international market.

Angelica (*Angelica sinensis*), *dong quai*, is known as the 'queen of women's herbs' and 'female ginseng' because it is used to regulate abnormal menstruation and to correct hot flushes. It is also used to treat appendicitis and rheumatism.

China-root (*Poria cocos*), *fu ling*, is a subterranean fungus, which grows on the roots of pine trees and is used as a tonic soup – especially for the elderly and infirm. Women in the Imperial Chinese court used this fungus to nourish the skin. Ci Xi, the last Empress of China, invented the famous *Poria* sandwich cake with a filling of honey, pine nuts and walnuts – a favourite with the Imperial concubines.

Chinese foxglove (*Rehmannia glutinosa*), *di huang*, roots are eaten as a food after steaming and mashing. The root is used in many ways as a herbal tonic, notably as an ingredient in 'Four Things Soup', together with *Angelica sinensis*, *Ligusticum wallichi* and *Paeonia lactiflora*, a woman's tonic widespread in China.

Chinese liquorice (*Glycyrrhiza uralensis*), *gan cao*, is a common Chinese herb, which disguises the taste of unpleasant medicines and makes medicinal components more effective.

Chinese yam (*Dioscorea opposita*), *shan yao*, is used as a food and as a digestive tonic. The root contains mucilage, which helps to soothe respiratory tubes and thereby ease breathing difficulties and coughs. It is also used to treat diabetes.

Chrysanthemum (*Chrysanthemum morifolium*), *ju hua*, dried flowers are brewed as a tea and used to alleviate hypertension and to lower cholesterol

levels. It generally detoxifies the body and purifies the blood and has some anti-viral and anti-bacterial properties. It aids recovery from influenza as a 'cooling' herb. The flowers are often combined with other herbs to treat childhood convulsions.

Cordyceps (*Cordyceps sinensis*), *dong chong xia cao*, is not a flowering plant but a caterpillar fungus. After the spores land on and infect a moth caterpillar, the parasitic fungus feeds on it until the fruiting body develops above ground; by then the caterpillar has died. It is collected mainly from upland pastures in Sichuan and Tibet and fetches a high price as an aphrodisiac.

Above:
Chinese herbal tea with flowers and fruits.

Dandelion (*Taraxacum officinale*), *pu gong ying*, is valuable as a diuretic and when combined with other herbs it is used to treat hepatitis and to enhance the immune response in upper respiratory tract infections. The white latex in the plant sap can be used to remove corns, warts and verrucae.

Eucommia (*Eucommia ulmoides*), *du zhong*, is a tree that produces white latex after the bark is cut. This is used to make medicines, given as a soup to lower blood pressure and cholesterol levels.

Ginger (*Zingiber officinalis*), *gan jiang*, rhizome is widely used as a spice in Chinese cuisine and to make a refreshing tea. Dried ginger is used for treating nausea and promoting blood circulation. Ginger may also ease joint pain from arthritis.

Ginseng, *ren shen*, is a famous Chinese herbal plant, used for over 4,000 years and referred to as the 'king of herbs', but only recognised in the West in the eighteenth century. The fleshy taproot treats many ailments, from cancer, diabetes and malaria, and is used as a general invigorating tonic, to improve blood circulation and treat hypertension. Chinese ginseng (*Panax ginseng*), *gao li shen*, was the original medicinal source, but now it is threatened by over-collection, and is widely cultivated in northern China. The related Siberian ginseng (*Eleutherococcus senticosus*), *chou shen*, has similar properties.

Ginkgo (*Ginkgo biloba*), *bai guo*, nut, found inside the fruit, is used in TCM after cooking to remove the toxins, to cure asthma and coughs. Gingko leaf extract is used to treat asthma, bronchitis and fatigue and recent studies have found that it helps to enhance the memory of elderly people.

Hemp (*Cannabis sativa*) leaves are well known as a narcotic drug, yet sufferers of multiple sclerosis use it to relieve the neuro-muscular problems associated with the disease. Hemp has been used in Chinese medicines for 6,000 years; today it is mainly the seeds, *huo ma ren*, that are roasted or boiled to prepare a tea. This helps to alleviate the symptoms of osteoporosis, Parkinson's and Alzheimer's diseases. In addition, it strongly increases the desire for food, which has been found to aid treatment of anorexia nervosa.

Lily (*Lilium lancifolium*) is used both as a food and as a mild medicine. Dried bulb portions, *bai hei*, are cooked in soups all year round. Fresh bulbs are eaten raw or lightly cooked. When taken with honey it moistens the lungs and alleviates coughing.

Lotus (*Nelumbo nucifera*) seeds or nuts, *lian zi*, are eaten raw as a snack, while dried seeds are cooked and mashed to form the lotus seed paste used as a filling for mooncakes, eaten at the autumn full moon festival. All parts of the plant are used medicinally: leaves for sunstroke and fever, seeds for insomnia, seed pods to treat cervical cancer and petals for syphilis. The entire plant counteracts the effects of mushroom poisoning.

Above:
Two of the descendents of the 26 Eld's deer, in Datian NR on Hainan Island, saved from extinction in China by a captive breeding programme begun in 1976.

land area. The aim is to increase the percentage to 16 per cent by 2010 and 17 per cent by 2020. However, the declaration of any area as a reserve does not automatically ensure it will be conserved; they need good management and protection from exploitation.

Several wetland species, which have been saved from the brink of extinction, are mentioned on p79. The Hainan subspecies of the rare Eld's deer (*Cervus eldii siamensis*), still survives there thanks to sterling efforts at Datian Nature Reserve (NR). In 1976 there were only 26 animals left in China, but by 2007 this had increased to some 1,600 head. In the early days, a female goat was used as a foster mother. Like many deer, it was killed for the antlers to be used as an aphrodisiac in TCM, but gradually the local people are being educated to refrain from hunting their special deer.

China produces more hydro power than any country and continues to build yet more of these power stations, but the dams present huge problems for aquatic life. Now, evidence of more eco-friendly renewable energy sources abounds: the rooftops of most city buildings are bristling with solar-powered water heaters and they are even used in remote parts of the countryside. China has two major windy regions; one of these is a vast area stretching from the north-west to the north-east and the other is on the east coast. In 2007, the largest wind power plant in China is at Dabancheng outside Urumqi.

Above:
Late in the day, sun beams onto a solar-powered water panel beside a Dai house backed by ancient tea terraces in southern Yunnan.

Below:
The largest wind power park in China is at Dabancheng outside Urumqii in Xinjiang Uygur AR.

Even though investment in the production of wind energy costs twice as much as coal-fired plants, China is committed to increasing the proportion of energy generated by wind, with a goal of 14 per cent of the global wind energy output by 2020. To this end, China's first offshore wind power station in Liaodong Bay in the north-east of the Bohai Sea began operation in November 2007. This is the first wind power station in the world to supply offshore oil and gas fields, replacing diesel and reducing the carbon dioxide and sulphur dioxide output. Two wind power facilities are also being built in Shanghai.

The State Environmental Protection Administration (SEPA) is responsible for protecting China's air, water and land from pollution and contamination. In addition, SEPA funds and organises research and development. The National Endangered Plant and Wildlife Protection and Nature Reserve Program (NCP) is a Chinese government initiative aimed at protecting China's biodiversity by improving existing reserves as well as establishing new ones. Managed by the State Forestry Administration, it provides stable funding for reserves, by improving their management and staff training, so that the reserves can work more efficiently, thereby benefiting the wildlife for future generations.

The WWF, whose panda logo was conceived by the late Sir Peter Scott, sponsored Chinese and Western scientists to work together towards the long-term goal of ensuring the survival of giant pandas in the wild. Indeed, WWF was the first

international conservation body to be invited to work with China. The WWF is currently involved in aiding conservation in China with their Living Yangtze Program (see p70) and the South China Wetlands Conservation Project which focuses on two wetland areas, one in Guangdong and the other in Fujian lying on the East Asian-Australasian Flyway where millions of waterbirds stopover to refuel during their annual migrations. The sites are also overwintering grounds for many other birds, some of which are endangered.

In November 2007, WWF together with TRAFFIC, (a joint programme of WWF and International Union for Conservation of Nature (IUCN), which monitors the trade in wild plants and animals to make sure it is not a threat to the conservation of nature) and a large advertising agency, launched a graphic media campaign in Beijing to tackle the problem of illegal wildlife trade. Other international organisations involved in conservation within China include the WCS which began its conservation work in China in the early 1980s when Dr George Schaller studied giant pandas in Sichuan and upland ungulates in Tibet AR. More recently, the WCS have been working with the Siberian tiger (*Panthera tigris altaica*) and the Chinese alligator (*Alligator sinensis*).

The Conservation International (CI) China Program was launched in 2002 and their focal area is the mountainous region of southwest China. Founded as recently as 1993, the China Environmental Protection Foundation (CEPF) is an NGO dedicated to protecting China's environment. It raises funds to sponsor environmental activities and projects; it also commends organisations and individuals that have made outstanding contributions to environmental protection.

Below:
Ecotourism at its best. Local fishermen, atop their bamboo rafts, perform in *Impression Sanjie Lui*, a light and sound extravaganza directed by the famous movie director Zhang Yimou, depicting local life at the open-air Li River Mountain-Water Theatre. This is the biggest natural stage in the world, sited at Yangshuo, Guilin in Guangxi Zhuang AR.

Ecotourism

New highways and much improved public transport systems have enabled tourism to develop rapidly in China today. New-found wealth in China has meant that huge numbers of people are travelling further afield within their own country and overseas tourists are increasing too. In 2006, China overtook Italy as the world's fourth most popular destination and it is not inconceivable that China will become number one by 2020. Well-worn routes to the Great Wall, Forbidden City and Terracotta Warriors are as popular as ever, especially for first-time visitors to China. However, as China begins to promote green tourism, the lure of seeing a live giant panda remains a high priority. Now specialised tours into wilder areas for plant-hunters and bird-watchers as well as naturalists, artists and photographers, are being promoted. Ecotourism is helping to raise the profile of conservation – both internationally and within China.

It may be too late to save the Yangtze river dolphin or *baiji* (*Lipotes vexillifer*) and the South China tiger (*Panthera tigris amoyensis*), but the efforts to rescue the Chinese alligator, Eld's deer and, more famously, the giant panda are looking much more hopeful. As environmental ethics gradually become established, it will be vital to increase awareness of wildlife conservation. Education – especially amongst China's younger generation – will doubtless play a key role towards achieving the aim of preserving a green China for future generations. The years ahead will be critical, but the opportunities are there for people and wildlife to co-exist more positively in the future.

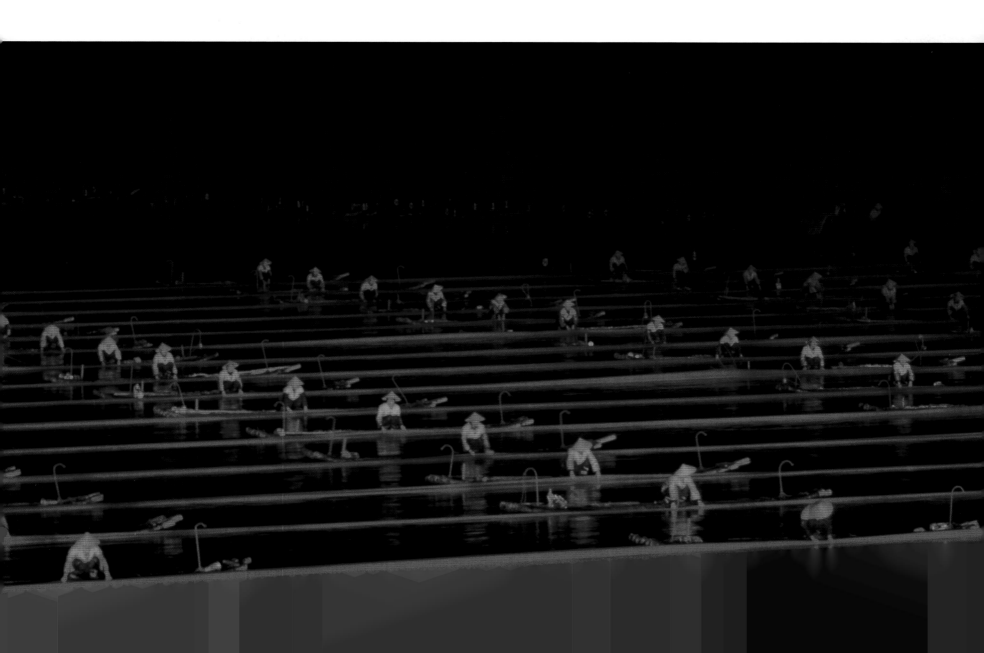

NATURE IN CHINESE ART

Traditional Chinese ink brush paintings are often inspired by nature, whether it is natural landscapes, wildlife or floral designs. Calligraphy greatly influenced this style and, indeed, may appear as part of the composition as a description or a poem. Using water-based black ink made from lampblack or tung oil, the pigments are compressed into a stick or a cake. Just before painting on paper or silk, the pigment is ground and mixed with water to produce fresh paint to create the so-called ink-and-wash paintings. The artist works entirely freehand using different sized brushes to create broad or narrow strokes with more or less ink to vary the intensity of the stroke. Most often an impression of nature is portrayed maybe with elements of a natural scene, such as mountains or rivers.

Another style of painting, known as blue-and-green landscapes, use blue, green and red mineral pigments to produce vivid coloured artworks. Later on, flower and bird paintings developed as a distinct genre, depicting not only birds and flowers, but also fruits, frogs, marine life and fish.

Three-dimensional miniature landscapes – known as *penjing* – developed as an art form in China in the Tang Dynasty. Inspired by nature and landscape paintings, *penjing* artists make their creations in a container by combining natural stone and plants to convey a mountain scene or an aquatic landscape. Careful selection of the colour, shape and size of rocks is crucial, as is the tree type, the growth form and number of plants; since they have to harmonise with each other to create a landscape as realistic as if the hand of Nature had created it.

During the nineteenth and much of the twentieth centuries, *penjing* declined as collections were lost or destroyed, so artists were unable to pass on their knowledge and skills. But over the last two decades, this ancient art has been revived and fine examples of *penjing* are displayed to perfection against a plain wall in public gardens. Bonsai – the art of growing diminutive trees in pots – developed later.

Within classical gardens, examples of plant and animal designs can be found in wall apertures, on carved shutters and as path mosaics. Cranes (a symbol of longevity), bats (a symbol of happiness) and lotus flowers (a symbol of purity and beauty) are frequently featured.

Paper cutting is a folk art practised all over China, where it originated thousands of years ago. The oldest known papercuts, found in Xinjiang Uygur AR, date from the Northern Dynasties period. Either sharp pointed scissors or a knife is used to make the cuts, which may be mono-coloured or multicoloured. The simplest

are made by folding the paper (usually black or red), once or several times so that after cutting it opens out into a symmetrical design. Other types of cuts are designs, which range from simple individual animals (such as signs of the Chinese zodiac) to elaborate scenes. Papercuts are used to decorate walls, windows and doors as well as lanterns.

An ephemeral art form, which is restricted to the severe winter months in Harbin, in the far north-west of China, is the creation of ice sculptures in celebration of the Chinese New Year. During the Qing Dynasty, local families used to make ice lanterns by partially freezing water in buckets, then boring a hole in the frozen shell to drain out the water, leaving a cavity for a candle. Now the sculptures have developed into elaborate structures on display in Zhaoling Park. Huge blocks of ice are cut from the Songhua River and carved into ambitious replicas of pagodas, bridges or even a downsized Great Wall, which glow at night from internal coloured lights. Smaller pieces glisten in the sunlight in China's ice city.

Butter sculptures are another ephemeral art form that has to be made in sub-zero temperatures to prevent the butter from melting. Originating from Lhasa in Tibet AR, the process of using yak butter was introduced to the Ta'er or

Kumbum Monastery in Xining at the beginning of the seventeenth century. It is here that the finest butter sculptures are displayed during the Yak Butter Lamp Festival on the fifteenth day of the Lunar New Year. The monks spend three months working in rooms in freezing temperatures sculpting the yak butter after dipping their hands in icy water. Old butter sculptures are combined with wheat ash to produce a black mixture that is moulded into shape as the base onto a bamboo framework. After a covering of fresh butter is applied, it is painted with mineral or vegetable dyes.

Left:
Plum blossom flowers early around the time of the Chinese New Year; so it is regarded as a symbol of renewal. It is not uncommon for snow to fall on these flowers, as depicted here, which signifies fortitude.

Opposite:
1. An example of a plant and animal study: carp swimming beneath lotus lilies. The red seal of the artist appears beneath the calligraphy characters.
2. An ink-and-wash painting of bamboo – one of four noble plants – conveys the essential features of this grass, the stem divided by nodes and the drooping leaves. The logo for the 2008 Beijing Olympics appears lower right.
3. Dragon ice sculptures are popular subjects in the outdoor annual Ice Festival at Harbin.
4. The Miao people in Guizhou produce colourful embroidered sleeve panels incorporating stylised plants and animals; this one portrays a silkworm dragon and phoenix-like birds.
5. Lotus flowers depicted in this papercut stand for purity and beauty.

Overleaf:
Thousands of locals and tourists converge on Ta'er Monastery each year to see the intricate yak butter sculptures. The figurines are depicted holding flowers or fruits as offerings to Buddha at a time of year when fresh flowers are unavailable.

1

2

5

Forests

The varied climate and extreme latitude range in China produce an exceptionally diverse range of forests – mostly in the east and south – which are home to most of the country's wildlife. Moving down from the north, cool taiga gives way to temperate coniferous and deciduous forests; followed by subtropical forests in slightly warmer climates, with tropical rainforests and mangroves in the far south. Bamboo forests, both natural and planted, also occur; whereas alpine forests cling precariously to exposed mountains.

In autumn, as birch and larch trees turn a glorious gold, they transform parts of Kanas NNR.

China's forests harbour many rare trees and associated rare and endangered animals and plants. However, meeting the need to feed a large proportion of the world's population (currently 22 per cent with 1.3 billion people) has been at the expense of the natural forests, with the result that China now has only four per cent of the world's forests.

The type of forest changes not only with latitude, but also with altitude; moving down a single mountain, the forest can change from a stunted coniferous alpine forest immediately below the snow line, to a coniferous forest, a mixed forest and, finally to an evergreen forest at a low altitude. Each forest type is outlined below, with descriptions of notable examples.

Taiga (or boreal) forests

The southern limit of the extensive cool-temperate forest that covers northern Eurasia extends into the north-eastern province of Heilongjiang and the north of Inner Mongolia AR (Da Hinggan or Da Xing'an Ling Range). The taiga clothes mountains where winters are prolonged and temperatures can plummet to −35°C. Most of the trees are conifers in this region where frost-free days total less than one third of the year. The dominant tree, the Dahurian larch (*Larix gmelinii*) sheds its needles before the onset of winter; whereas both the Korean spruce (*Picea koraiensis*) and Mongolian scots pine (*Pinus sylvestris* var. *mongolica*) retain their needles. Interspersed amongst the conifers are several deciduous broadleaf trees including Mongolian oak (*Quercus mongolica*), David's poplar (*Populus davidiana*) and two northern birch species, (Manchurian, *Betula platyphylla* and Dahurian, *B. davurica*). As trees fall and gaps appear in the canopy, the deciduous broadleaf trees grow up first, with the Dahurian larch reappearing only when there is sufficient shade. For this reason, secondary forest in the area consists mostly of broadleaf trees. Mosses and lichens flourish in this damp forest and where light reaches the forest floor, the ground-hugging shrub, cowberry (*Vaccinium vitis-idaea*), produces attractive red fruits that are harvested for jam.

Brown bear (*Ursus arctos*), red deer (*Cervus elaphus*), moose (*Alces alces*), musk deer (*Moschus moschiferus*) and wolverine (*Gulo gulo*) are some of the mammals which are quite common here; rarer inhabitants are the endangered Siberian tiger and sable (*Martes zibellina*). Birds, such as the hazel grouse (*Bonasa bonasia*) and various finches also live here.

Above:
Pendulous male and erect female catkins of Asian white birch (*Betula platyphylla*).

Opposite:
Autumn colours on the Beijing Hills seen from the Great Wall.

Opposite below:
Cowberry fruits are collected from Changbai Shan for making jam and wine.

Right:
Brown bears roam through China's northern forests.

Coniferous forests

Temperate coniferous forests include conifers such as the Korean pine (*Pinus koraiensis*) and Siberian larch (*Larix sibirica*). Extensive coniferous forests of spruce and fir cover the Altai and Tian mountains in Xinjiang Uygur AR.

Changbai Mountains Man and Biosphere Programme (MAB) on the border of Jilin with North Korea, contains the richest forests in north-east China and is one of only two primaeval Korean pine forests in China. The other is on the Lesser Xing'an Mountains in the north-east of Heilongjiang. On a fine day in June, the whole forest at Changbai Shan erupts with copious yellow clouds of microscopic Korean pine pollen grains wafting in the wind pollinating erect female cones. When ripe Korean fir cones are eaten by Eurasian red squirrels (*Sciurus vulgaris*), this helps to disperse the seeds.

Kanas Lake NNR lies at the northern edge of the Altai Mountains not far from the border with Kazakhstan. Apart from the lake itself, the main attraction is the forest, which surrounds the lake. This, the southernmost limit of the Eurasian boreal forest, looks more like northern Europe than China. Here deciduous Siberian larch and birches intermingle with evergreen Siberian spruce (*Picea obovata*). In October, when the overnight temperatures plummet, the green chlorophyll in the deciduous larch needles and birch leaves breaks down forming yellow pigments in the leaves and needles that paint the forest with radiant splashes of gold. Amongst the endangered animals which occur here are snow leopard (*Uncia uncia*), wolverine, brown bear, otter (*Lutra lutra*) and Eurasian lynx (*Lynx lynx*).

Above:
Wolves (*Canis lupus*) are agile forest predators.

Above right:
The Eurasian red squirrel lives in northern forests.

Opposite above:
Roscoea tibetica grows up through pine needles in Yunnan.

Opposite below:
Conifers on the road from Haba to Zhongdian in Yunnan.

Right:
Detail of the facial disc of an Eurasian eagle owl (*Bubo bubo*).

PANDAS

Left:
A panda sits feeding against the natural mountain backdrop at Wolong in Sichuan.

Opposite:
1. A giant panda loses its footing and slides down a snowy slope at Wolong in February.

2. Regardless of the weather, giant pandas need to feed throughout the year. Even at the lowest levels of their distribution, snow falls on several days each winter, but their thick oily pelts provide an effective insulation against the cold and are also waterproof. To help conserve energy, pandas sit or even lie down to feed.

3. Pausing on a walk beside the Pitiao River at Wolong, a giant panda is reflected in a pool.

4. A young giant panda plays from a high vantage point in a pine tree.

5. A mixed forest meets the edge of the tumbling Pitiao River in Wolong NNR.

6. A four-month-old baby panda cub looks at its mother for reassurance in the panda breeding centre at Wolong.

7. The red panda also known as firefox, is more widespread and less endangered than the giant panda. Feeding also on bamboo, the diet is varied by eating bird eggs and nestlings. Red pandas have a long bushy tail, which is used as an effective duvet during the winter.

Mountain peaks which appear and disappear in swirling clouds, babbling brooks, clear blue lakes, flowering rhododendrons, fiery autumnal hues and snow-covered bamboo groves are just some of the seasonal cameos within the panda's home territory. Fossil evidence shows giant pandas once lived in forests from Burma (Myanmar) in the south up to Peking (Beijing) in the north. Forest destruction for agriculture, as well as logging and poaching, have pushed the pandas northwards. Now, the total wild population of some 1,600 pandas is confined to the Qinling and Min Mountains on the eastern edge of the Tibetan Plateau in just three provinces – Sichuan, Shaanxi and Gansu. Living in a zone between 1,200 and 3,500 metres above sea level, giant pandas inhabit biologically diverse regions whose fauna includes red pandas (*Ailurus fulgens*) and golden snub-nosed monkeys (*Rhinopithecus roxellana*).

Long before pandas were given as diplomatic gifts, Chinese emperors kept pandas as part of their menagerie. But these enchanting monochromatic mammals with their eyes enhanced by black eye patches set within a white face, were unknown to the western world until Père Armand David spotted a skin in 1869. It was to be another 68 years before a live panda was brought out of China and exhibited at Chicago Zoo.

Giant pandas have retained a short carnivorous gut, although they now feed almost exclusively on bamboo. Arrow bamboo (*Sinarundinaria fangiana*) and umbrella bamboo (*Fargesia robusta*) are their favourite species, which varies with the seasons, as pandas move down the mountains in winter and up again in the spring. Because the bamboo is not digested efficiently, a panda has to consume 12 to 38 kilos each day – just to stay alive. So, unlike brown bears, pandas cannot hibernate because they are unable to lay down enough fat reserves.

Great strides have been made in panda conservation in recent years with the banning of logging and the declaration of over 40 reserves; although some are small isolated pockets. The recent planting of bamboo corridors to link up some reserves is beneficial in several ways: it increases the gene pool and also encourages the pandas to move into new areas to feed. The bamboo they feed on grows for many years until all the plants of a species in one area flower at the same time and die. This synchronous flowering provides an abundance of bamboo seed, which ensures plentiful bamboo seedlings to replace the dead groves, but can be a serious problem for the pandas. With more expansive territories, pandas used to simply amble off to a new bamboo grove, hence the benefit of bamboo corridors to link up smaller reserves.

Since the first captive panda birth in 1963, the number of cubs born in captivity each year has markedly increased. In 2006, the first panda was released into the wild fitted with a radio collar. Less than a year later it was found dead; the damaged body indicated it probably died by falling off a precipice after fighting another male.

Mixed forests

Mixed forests of broadleaved and coniferous trees occur where there are distinct warm and cool seasons; the species mix varies with climate and altitude. These forests occur on Changbai Shan, on the Central China loess plateau and on the Huang Hue Plain.

On Changbai Mountains below 1,100 metres, mixed stands of conifers intermingle with deciduous broadleaf trees such as oak, ash, birch and the Amur linden (*Tilia amurensis*) – the leaves of which are eaten as a famine food. Two species of *Actinidia* occur here; the Chinese gooseberry is a woody climber which is cultivated and marketed so successfully in New Zealand as kiwi fruit; and *Actinidia kolomikta*. This is an attractive ornamental climber, with a curious mix of white or pink-tipped leaves that scrambles up to ten metres off the ground in glades or along stream banks where some light penetrates down through the overhead canopy in its natural habitat. The medicinal plant ginseng (*Panax ginseng*) grows here, but over-zealous collection has made it an endangered wild plant. Above this zone is a sombre coniferous forest with species that originate from Siberia, western Eurasia, Korea and Japan. These conifers are festooned with epiphytic mosses, while various ferns, flowering plants and grasses grow on the floor below. Still higher, the variety of conifers is reduced. Both hazel grouse and black grouse (*Lyrurus tetrix*) live in these forests. Changbai Mountains are also an important breeding site for the scaley-sided merganser (*Mergus squamatus*) – which nests in tree holes.

The Central China Loess Plateau, infamous for its disastrous floods caused by erosion and deposition of the fine soil, has little original forest left intact. Extensive logging, grazing and agriculture have degraded the forests to such an extent that secondary growth is now more extensive than the original forest. Heavy grazing, in particular, encourages the spread of thorny shrubs such as *Caragana*. Some afforestation has taken place; for the most part with fruit trees and monocultures – not so attractive for wildfe as original native species. Finer than sand, loess is one of the most erosion-prone soils known on Earth. Successful prevention of erosion of these fragile soils requires the right mix of species to be planted to produce ecologically balanced plantations, which are also economically viable.

The Huang Hue Plain has been farmed for many centuries, so much of the original mixed forests have been eliminated. The natural vegetation of the Shandong Peninsula, was once dominated by deciduous oaks, with elm, pistachio (*Pistacia*

Above top:
White fruits and red leaves of Chinese mountain ash (*Sorbus hupehensis*) in Jiuzhaigou, Sichuan.

Above:
A mosaic of autumn colours includes *Cotinus* shrubs at Juizhaigou, Sichuan.

Left:
For a few brief days in early spring, deciduous trees leaf out to transform the lower slopes in Wolong NNR with acid yellow, bronze and pale green hues.

Above:
A primaeval forest grows from a mossy carpet at 3,030 metres. This forest has survived intact despite extensive logging in the 1970s at Jiuzhaigou, Sichuan.

Right:
Mosses grow on logs inside the humid primaeval forest at Jiuzhaigou.

Far right:
The flaking bark of birch (*Betula albo-sinensis*) in Jiuzhaigou, Sichuan.

Left:
In cold weather, rhododendron leaves unfurl and hang down, Wolong NNR.

Below:
Bamboo leaves weighed down with snow at Wolong NNR.

Opposite above:
Dhole or Asiatic wild dogs (*Cuon alpinus*) live and hunt in packs and will attack young giant pandas.

Opposite below:
As a young golden snub-nosed monkey leaps from one tree to another, it uses the tail as a rudder.

Opposite far right:
A golden snub-nosed monkey mother cradles her baby, Sichuan.

chinensis), and the conifer (*Pinus tabulaeformis*), but has been replaced by a secondary cover of red pine (*Pinus densiflora*). The peninsula is a nesting area for seabirds including the splendid white-tailed sea eagle (*Haliaeetus albicilla*).

The forest which covers the upper levels of the mountains rising up from Jiuzhaigou (Nine Village Gorge) in the Min Shan mountain range in Sichuan is coniferous. Lower down, a distinct banding of forest type can be seen as the road ascends the mountain. From 2,000 to 2,700 metres there is a montane mixed forest; predominately pine and oak forest below a fir and spruce forest. Amongst this, some of the finest autumn colours are to be found, with the red leaves of Chinese mountain ash off-setting the white fruits, plus the fiery red smoke tree (*Cotinus coggyria*) dominant on the south-facing slopes and various maples (*Acer* spp.) adding to the colourful mosaic. Higher still, extending up to 3,500 metres is a cloud forest dominated initially by fountain bamboo (*Fargesia nitida*) – an important food of giant pandas – with rhododendrons higher up. There are also spruce forests on the sunny slopes and fir forests on the shady ones. The lack of firs on the south-facing slopes was initially thought to be a climatic factor but it has now been discovered that in Jiuzhaigou the forest gradually became reduced by herders felling the trees to increase the area of pasture on the best slopes for grazing their animals.

At the end of Rize Gully, which branches off Jiuzhaigou, there is a primaeval forest at an altitude of 3,060 metres which survived the extensive logging of the 1970s. In this mature ecosystem, old-growth firs and spruces rise up from a lush mossy carpet in a forest where the temperature remains cool even at mid-day in summer. Finally, from 3,500 to 3,800 metres the subalpine forest zone has firs on the shady slopes and juniper on the sunny slopes.

Living in these forest, but rarely seen, are the giant and red pandas together with other mammals of oriental origin including golden snub-nosed monkeys, takin (*Budorcas taxicolor*), tufted deer (*Elaphodus cephalophus*), serow (*Capricornis sumatrensis*) and bamboo rat (*Rhizomys sinensis*) as well as mammals originating from the East Tibet Palaearctic region such as the Asiatic black bear (*Ursus thibetanus*), goral (*Neamorhedus goral*) and white-lipped deer (*Cervus albirostris*). Notable birds at Jiuzhaigou include blue-eared pheasants, Sichuan jays (*Perisoreus internigrans*) and Sichuan wood owls (*Strix davidi*).

To the south-west of Jiuzhaigou, lies the famous Wolong MAB at the transition between the Sichuan temperate and the Tibetan frigid zones. Wolong has high mountains and deep valleys ranging in elevation from 1,200 to 6,525 metres above sea level on the eastern slopes of the Qionglai Mountains. Summer weather is cloudy

and humid because of the influence of the moisture-laiden south-west monsoons. This, the largest and most important of all the panda reserves, has an outstandingly rich biodiversity of plants and animals – many of which are rare or endangered. On the lower slopes, a variety of deciduous and evergreen broadleaf trees – including maples, rhododendrons, magnolias and tree peonies – intermingle with conifers, and the pandas' life-giving bamboos. During the last Ice Age, this area was never totally glaciated and so became a refuge for a rich assortment of endemic plants, some of which have survived from the Mesozoic era. There is the dove or pocket handkerchief tree, the Katsura tree (*Cercidophyllum japonicum*), the dawn redwood (*Metasequoia glyptostroboides*) and the endangered gingko or maidenhair tree. As the elevation increases, more conifers begin to appear.

In addition to giant pandas, wildlife in this reserve includes the red panda, the golden snub-nosed monkey, snow and clouded leopards, the dhole or Asiatic wild dog and no fewer than fifteen different kinds of pheasants.

M ale pheasants sport colourful and strikingly patterned feathers, often with long showy tails, which make them popular birds amongst ornamental collections in the West. Females, on the other hand, tend to have a drab cryptic colouration that blends in well with the ground vegetation when sitting on their nests. China is home to seventeen pheasant species, including the ring-necked pheasant (*Phasianus colchicus*). It is now widespread in Europe and North America as a game bird after being introduced from China around 4 BC.

The male golden pheasant (*Chrysolophus pictus*) is one of the most gaudy of all pheasants with a spectacular mix of golden, green, blue and reddish-brown feathers. Endemic to central China, it lives on scrubby hillsides and in secondary forests. The male courts his mate with an elaborate display by leaping up and twisting his body in mid-air. The golden and black nape ruff of the male is not unlike the white nape feathers edged in black of the male Lady Amherst's pheasant (*Chrysolophus amherstiae*) and together they are known as ruffed pheasants.

All four species of eared pheasants (*Crossoptilon* spp.) have a tuft of feathers projecting upwards behind each eye, a bare red orbital area around the eye and red feet. They live in small flocks at high altitudes. The white-eared pheasant (*C. crossoptilon*) lives on the south-east Tibetan Plateau at 3-4,000 metres along the treeline. Most of the body is white apart from the flight feathers and the floppy tail, which are both black. The Tibetan eared pheasant (*C. harmani*) is similar in stance and size but has blackish wings. In both, the ear-tufts are not so pronounced as in blue and brown-eared pheasants (*C. mantchuricum*).

The green peafowl (*Pavo muticus*), known as the dragonbird, was once widespread in Yunnan's southern forests. Loss of habitat, as well as hunting for food, have reduced the numbers of this most splendid of all the pheasant family. As the peacock moves, the magnificent iridescent hues of the tail feathers shimmer as the light changes.

Male peacock pheasants have showy eyespots on their tails, which are displayed to the females by fanning out the tail as well as raising up the wings. The grey peacock pheasant (*Polyplectron bicalcaratum*), occurs in montane evergreen forest in western and southern Yunnan and also in Tibet AR. Rarer still is the small Hainan peacock pheasant (*P. katsumatae*), which is restricted to Hainan Island.

Also included in the pheasant family are the tragopans. Instead of using tail ornaments to attract a female, the males display by expanding their wattles with one wing lowered and the other raised. Male Temminck's tragopan (*Tragopan temminckii*) and Cabot's tragopan (*T. caboti*) both display a bright blue and red patterned throat wattle and erect blue 'horn' wattles.

Striking pheasant feathers have been used in many ways. Original Chinese fans were made from feathers and a pheasant fan is known to date back to the Shang Dynasty. Peacock feathers – which are shed annually – were also used to make magnificent feather fans, which became used as decorations by emperors from the Western Han Dynasty.

During the Warring States Period two pheasant feathers were placed in the generals' headgear to signify boldness and courage on the battlefield. Pheasant tail feathers are still used as head-dresses today. Several minority groups perform the lusheng dance wearing silver horns and colourful pheasant feathers on their heads. The 1.5-metre-long tail feathers of male Reeves pheasants (*Syrmaticus reevesii*) are used as head decorations in the traditional Beijing opera.

The main threat to these glorious pheasants is loss of their natural habitat, together with illegal hunting for food in some areas.

Left:
A green peacock with tail held erect during courtship.

Opposite:
1. The resplendent male golden pheasant perches in a conifer.

2. During courtship, the green peacock attracts a peahen by erecting his long tail coverts and shimmers the iridescent eyespots at the feather tips.

3. A male Temminck's tragopan inflates his spectacular throat lappets to woo his mate.

4. Silver pheasants (*Lophura nycthemera*) live in evergreen forests and bamboo thickets in southern China, where they home in to feed on figs dropped by monkeys and doves. This male shows the distinct long white tail.

5. The blue-eared pheasant (*Crossoptilon auritum*) is bluish-grey with long white 'ear' tufts. It frequents dwarf mountain forest.

6. Male grey peacock pheasant displays to the female by bowing and raising the splayed out wings with the dramatic violet-green eyespots.

7. Detail of grey peacock pheasant feathers showing iridescent eye spots.

Below:
Brightly coloured contour feathers of cock ring-necked pheasant.

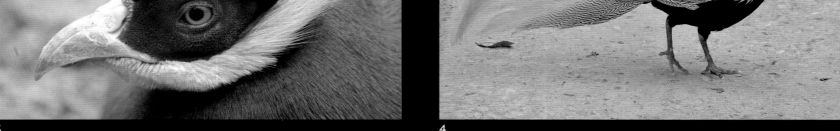

Deciduous forests

Much of China was once covered with deciduous forests, but most were cleared some 5,000 years ago for agriculture. A few remnants remain in north-east, central and south-west China. These forests grow at elevations midway between the upper coniferous forest and the lower tropical forests.

Several trees of commercial value grow in this zone – the walnut (*Juglans regia*), the sweet chestnut (*Castanea sativa*) and persimmon (*Diospryros kaki*). If not picked, the latter will retain the conspicuous orange fruits long after the leaves have fallen; it belongs to the same genus as ebony, but its wood is not prized to the same extent.

These forests no longer harbour large mammals; those that do occur, are the same types as are present in Western deciduous forests, such as squirrels and voles.

Subtropical evergreen broadleaf forests

Evergreen oaks and laurels, together with trees belonging to the tea family are widespread in subtropical evergreen forests with bamboos as the under storey. On Hainan Island, subtropical evergreen forests occur on the coastal plains with monsoon forests on domed mountains in the interior. Many of the camellias cultivated in Western gardens for their large showy flowers originate from China; but the most famous of all the camellias must surely be the tea tree. Tea is harvested

Above top:
Azure-winged magpies (*Cyanopica cyana*) often move through forests in groups.

Above:
The lacebark pine (*Pinus bungeana*), which is cultivated for its attractive flaking bark, naturally occurs in north-east and central China.

Opposite top:
Tea produces small white flowers.

Opposite centre:
Persimmon fruit remain on the tree after the leaves have fallen and have a high sugar content.

Opposite below:
Male golden pheasant – one of the many pheasants found in Wolong NNR.

Above right:
Fruit of the Chinese plum yew (*Cephalotaxus fortunei*), was collected by Robert Fortune.

by plucking the new growth shoots which maintains the bushes at a convenient height – around a metre. If left to grow unchecked, wild tea trees can reach ten metres high. Tea – known as *ch'a* in parts of China – has been drunk in this country from the first millennium BC but did not reach Europe until the seventeenth century. Tea was so highly esteemed in China, some Emperors planted wild tea tree gardens in appreciation of the refreshing drink.

The camphor tree (*Cinnamomum camphora*) is a broadleaved aromatic evergreen that grows in southern China. It can reach 15-30 metres in height with a huge canopy that is twice as wide as it is high. The timber is especially useful for making trunks for storing woollen garments, because the camphor oil deters clothes moths. Large numbers of ancient camphor trees can be seen in Xiaoqi, a village with narrow streets and houses that date back to the Ming and Qing Dynasties in Wuyuan County (Zhejiang).

In Maolan Karst Forest Nature Reserve (Guizhou) there is a bizarre and rare primaeval subtropical forest, where the trees somehow manage to grow on rocks with virtually no soil. Fallen leaves wedged in crevices provide humus where water accumulates. Even so, the trees take a long time to grow and so are short and thin. The local ethnic people used to earn a living by collecting wood to make charcoal, but now it is illegal to cut the trees or hunt the animals they are given financial help if wild animals destroy their crops.

Left:
Part of the tropical rainforest in Wild Elephant Valley, Xishuangbanna NNR, Yunnan, in the dry season.

Below:
A tropical rainforest strangler fig grapples its host tree in Xishuangbanna.

Opposite top:
Woody lianas scramble up and over rainforest trees in Xishuangbanna.

Opposite below:
The diminutive lesser mouse deer (*Tragulus javanicus*), which is China's smallest deer and weighs less than two kilograms, lives in forests in south Yunnan.

Tropical rainforests

South of the Tropic of Cancer tropical rainforests flourish where the monsoon climate maintains high average annual temperatures of 20-26.5°C. This, the smallest zone in China, is richer in number of species than any other. There are two types of tropical rainforests – tropical and monsoon. Tropical rainforest trees retain their leaves throughout the year; whereas in monsoon rainforest the trees lose their leaves during the dry season from November to March. This opens up the canopy so that the sunlight reaches the forest floor. Monsoon rainforests have fewer woody climbers or lianas than rainforests. Some trees, such as figs (*Ficus* spp.) have broad buttress roots extending out from the trunk. Only small areas of tropical rainforest with lush, dense jungles remain in south-west Yunnan and south-east Tibet AR. Much of the forest in southern Yunnan has been replaced with a monoculture of rubber (*Hevea brasiliensis*) plantations. Within the tropical rainforest there are three distinct layers: the shrub layer grows up above the herb layer with the tree canopy exposed to the sunlight. Epiphytic plants thrive in these forests; perching high up in forks or on branches of trees is a multitude of ferns and orchids, sending down aerial roots.

Strangler figs also start life high up trees when their seeds are left in bird droppings. After germination, roots grow down wrapping themselves around the trunk of their host tree. Eventually stranglers kill their host and are strong enough to stand on their own. Tropical edible fruits which originate from the rainforest are the lychee (*Litchi chinensis*), mangosteen (*Garcinia mangostana*), jack fruit (*Artocarpus hetereophyllus*) and longan (*Euphoria longa*) which is more cold resistant than lychee.

These rainforests are inhabited by gibbons (*Hylobates* spp.) that swing with great agility through the trees. Rhesus macaques (*Macaca mulatta*) run along branches,

frequently descending to the ground to drink or move through the forest. Another rainforest primate is the Phayre's leaf monkey (*Trachypithecus phayrei*), an arboreal leaf-eating species, that feeds early in the morning and late in the afternoon. It has unusually enlarged salivary glands that help to break down the plant material. Infant leaf monkeys have a striking orange coat, which gradually fades to the adult grey-brown.

In Xishuangbanna NNR Asian elephants migrate into Wild Elephant Valley during the wet season when it is possible to view them from an elevated walkway that allows the elephants to walk beneath. This reserve is also one of the last strongholds of the

Above left:
The blue tiger butterfly (*Tirumala limniace*) feeds on Lantana flowers, Yunnan.

Left:
A butterfly feeds on elephant urine in Wild Elephant Valley, Yunnan.

Above top:
The root of tiger's whisker (*Tacca chantrieri*), *lou hu xi*, is used in Chinese medicine.

Above centre:
Tropical mangosteen fruits are becoming popular in China.

Above:
Mucuna sempervirens is an evergreen woody climber, which produces purple flowers directly on the woody stems, Yunnan.

Opposite:
Common tiger butterfly (*Danaus genutia*) feeds on Lantana flowers, Yunnan.

BAMBOO

Bamboos are the most versatile of any group of evergreen plants. These woody, perennial grasses grow naturally in many countries but nowhere are they utilised more efficiently than China, where they are known as *zhu*. Here, bamboos have provided shelter, food, a source of fuel and a means of transport plus countless cooking utensils from chopsticks to rice steamers. Leisurely moments out in the open were enjoyed using bamboo products: whether fishing, flying kites or painting. From the sixteenth century BC, the earliest form of books in China was made using split bamboo strips, the only snag being some were so heavy that they had to be moved in a cart!

The most extensive bamboo forests occur in tropical and subtropical climates, where they thrive, but some species are able to grow in temperate regions. Stems of bamboo – known as culms – are selectively harvested from natural bamboo forests such as the South Sichuan Bamboo Sea or Shunan Zhuhai, which covers 120 square kilometres of mountain slopes at an elevation from 600 to 1,000 metres. Within this natural forest 30 different bamboos grow to provide a biodiverse habitat for other plants and wildlife. It is also the haunt of the much prized bamboo fungus (*Dictyophora indusiata*) which is collected and sold both as fresh and dried food.

Anji bamboo forest or Dazhuhai in Anhui on the other hand, was created in 1999 with pure stands of the giant timber moso bamboo (*Phyllostachys pubescens*) and has yet to develop its full potential as a tourist forest park. Here little direct light pierces the huge leafy crowns to reach the forest floor so hardly anything grows beneath them. This is a popular place for filmmakers; indeed it was one of the locations for the film *Crouching Tiger Hidden Dragon*. Moso plants are capable of reaching over 20 metres in height and the young culms can grow as much as a metre or more a day. Mature bamboo culms can be harvested after only five years, which is a big advantage over even fast-growing softwoods.

Bamboo plants regularly feature in ink brush paintings and even in the garden bamboos were not overlooked. Decorative species with attractive coloured stems – such as yellow and green striped and even black – are sought after as ornamental plants. Some bamboos have aesthetic qualities too, such as the curvaceous stem of the zig-zag bamboo (*Phyllostachys flexuosa*).

Succulent shoots (*zhu sun*) and dried bamboo stem sections are a regular part of any Chinese diet. The giant and red panda feed almost exclusively on the leaves, shoots and tender stems of bamboo, while the underground rhizomes are the food of bamboo rats.

Large bamboo stems are lightweight and naturally strengthened with silica and lignin. When treated they form a very hard wood used to make scaffolding, fences, bridges, rafts and other boats. Amongst the countless household objects that have been made of bamboo are baskets, bowls, matting, blinds, furniture, food steamers, toys, and now bamboo yarn and fabric is available.

Many products have been replaced by plastic, although in today's conservation conscientious world, biodegradable bamboo is becoming popular again. In recent years, with the demand for bamboo floor-covering increasing both in China and abroad, the output of bamboo has risen substantially.

1

2

6

7

3

5

4

large dark-coated ox known as gaur (*Bos gaurus*). Birds are plentiful in rainforests and amongst the most spectacular are the parrots and hornbills, the jungle fowl, the green peafowl and the grey peacock pheasant. Multi-coloured butterflies weave their way through the forest until they find either a place to drink, or fruits and flowers to refuel by sipping nectar. Colourful frogs are common but are more difficult to spot.

Between 1950 and 1980 half of Hainan Island's forest cover was felled for planting sugar and rubber, but tropical rainforests still cover mountains in the highlands. Notable sites are Jianfengling NNR (which has been enlarged almost threefold since its designation) and Diaoluoshan National Rainforest Park (NRP) noted for more than 100 waterfalls within the tropical primæval forest. Hainan has been isolated from the mainland for a million years which has resulted in the evolution of several species unique to this island.

Opposite far left:
Chinese white cheeked gibbons (*Hylobates leucogenys*) use their outsized arms to swing from one tree to another, Yunnan.

Opposite left:
Phayre's leaf monkey has unusually large salivary glands which assist in breaking down the monkey's diet of tough leaves.

Opposite below left:
A rhesus macaque monkey checks it is safe to drink. Macaque frequently move thorugh the forest on the ground.

Right:
The green peacock is one of the most splendid of all the rainforest birds. Here, a male calls during the breeding season in Yunnan.

Far right:
A new fern frond begins to unfurl in Jianfengling NNR.

Below right:
The oriental pied-hornbill (*Anthracoceros albirostris*) has an outsized bill with a casque on top, which is surprisingly light since the inside is honeycombed. This hornbill feeds on fruit as well as insects and lizards.

Living fossils

Among China's many unusual trees is a handful which are especially interesting because they are living relics of fossil genera. The dawn redwood was considered to be extinct until it was discovered in 1941 growing in Hubei. This deciduous conifer, with shaggy cinnamon coloured bark, produces pale green feather-like leaves each spring, which before they fall, turn an attractive reddish-brown colour, not unlike the pelt of a red fox. It is a fast-growing tree that is easily propagated and is now widely planted along roadsides in China. It has also become a popular tree in parks and larger gardens in the West.

The ginkgo or maidenhair tree is another sole surviving species of an ancient group of trees, commonly found as a fossil. It, too, was thought to be extinct, until it

was found growing in Zhejiang in Tian Mu Shan Reserve. Considered to be a sacred tree in the East, some of the largest ginkgo trees grow alongside Buddhist temples and monasteries. They are deep-rooted and so can withstand strong winds or snow; most of the trees usually reach up to heights of 35 metres, but exceptionally, up to over 50 metres. A few trees are thought to be over 2,500 years old. Like yews and hollies, ginkgo trees are either male or female, so seeds cannot be produced unless a male tree

Above:
A boulder-strewn river cuts through the tropical rainforest in Jianfengling NNR on Hainan Island.

Above right:
An alert brown tree frog or Hong Kong whipping frog (*Polypedates megacephalus*), on Hainan Island.

grows close to a female one. The latter produce yellow fruits that smell of rancid butter when crushed; for this reason, male ginkgos are selected for planting as street trees in China and Japan. The nearest relatives of this living fossil date back 160 million years to the Permian period. As well as the ornamental value of the tree, ginkgo nuts are eaten in China whilst the leaves and fruits are used medicinally; so perhaps, not surprisingly, it is the national tree of China.

THE SIBERIAN TIGER

The Siberian tiger (*Panthera tigris altaica*) is the largest tiger in the world, with the males reaching up to three metres long and weighing up to 364 kilos. Also known as the Amur tiger, it lives in the Russian Far East (RFE) and northern China which both have very harsh winters. A thick layer of fat and long fur enable these tigers to survive temperatures to –30°C.

The natural habitat in the RFE is a mixed temperate boreal forest in mountains, which are blanketed by snow in winter. Outsized paws help to spread the tiger's weight by functioning like snowshoes. The Siberian tiger shares this forest with other predators such as the Far Eastern leopard, European lynx, wolverine and bears; so saving the tiger's habitat will help these as well as other animals and plants.

The fate of the Siberian tiger in China is inextricably linked with the RFE where it faces many threats – including loss of habitat to fire, logging and human settlement. Local people also compete to hunt the same prey, which typically includes deer and wild boar (*Sus scrofa*). Each tiger needs a territory (some 40 square kilometres) to hunt its prey, which is thin on the ground and if they fail to find it, they will take dogs from villages. Logging roads not only fragment the tiger's territory, but also make the forest more accessible to illegal poachers.

In the 1940s hunting for tiger parts – notably the skin, bones and penises (which have been used in traditional Chinese medicine for centuries in the belief that some of the strength and virility of the largest cat will be passed on) reduced the total population of the RFE Amur tiger to just 40. But anti-poaching efforts by Russians, with support from the WWF and other bodies, enabled the tigers to gradually recover, so that a 1995-96 survey organised by the WCS found 330-371 adult tigers and 100 cubs in the RFE. A decade later, a winter survey involving 1,000 field workers from several organisations, travelling on foot, skis or snowmobiles to count tiger tracks, found the tiger population was stable with 334-417 adults and 97-112 cubs.

Since 1995, it has been illegal for individuals to possess a gun in China, but tigers still get caught in snares and are shot in the RFE. After recent political and economic upheavals in Russia virtually all the NGOs which funded crack anti-poaching patrols under the umbrella Inspection Tiger pulled out after the government ceased to grant them authority to search and charge poachers. The tigers could be saved in the RFE if bigger reserves were set up with proper protection.

Now that the South China tiger (*Panthera tigris amoyensis*) is thought to be ecologically extinct, the Siberian tiger is the only wild tiger remaining in China, where it is thought there are currently around 20 individuals, and efforts are being made to aid their comeback. The WCS is one of the few organisations working on the Amur tiger in China, where it began tiger surveys in 1998. It provided support to set up the Hunchun NR in Jilin on the west side of the RFE/China border, providing a corridor for tigers to move into China and repopulate regions where they used to roam.

The WCS undertake surveys and research, as well as supporting Hunchun NR and four forestry bureaux with their anti-poaching patrols, by using local staff and volunteers to eliminate snares, over 10,000 have been removed. Local media publicity helped to raise awareness of the plight of the tiger, which is, after all, one of the twelve signs of the Chinese zodiac. From 2000-2005, WCS provided half of the value of the livestock lost to tigers to compensate the local community. Since 2006, Jilin Government has taken over the compensation. The WCS is also engaged in making local people and school children more aware of the need to conserve the few remaining tigers in their country.

Captive-bred Siberian tigers abound in China. There are 700 alone at the Feline Breeding Centre at Harbin, but until their safety can be guaranteed, releasing them into the wild cannot be an option.

1

2

5

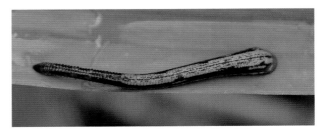

The dove or pocket handkerchief tree has striking inflorescences; the small flowers are grouped into a spherical head surrounded by a pair of white bracts that flutter in the breeze resembling doves or handkerchiefs. E.H. Wilson, who collected seed of this tree, describes in his journal how the bracts are most conspicuous on dull days and early in the morning. He regarded *Davidia involucrata* as the most interesting and beautiful of all trees within the north-temperate flora.

The evergreen conifer, Cathay silver fir (*Cathaya argyrophylla*) was discovered in Huaping National Park as recently as 1955 growing at 950-1,800 metres on precipitous cliffs, which are swathed in fog for much of the year. It was identified as a new species in a new genus named from Cathay, the old name for China, and the needle-like leaves that resemble a fir with two silver bands on their underside. The Cathay silver fir is a relic plant from the Tertiary period. Initially, the seeds of this silver fir did not germinate well in cultivation and only a few of the seedlings which did germinate actually survived. After years of research and experimentation, biologists have managed to raise the germination rate from four to ninety per cent. It is hoped that ways will be found to encourage this slow-growing fir to grow faster so that it can be propagated and, like the ginkgo, dawn redwood and handkerchief tree, eventually be distributed for planting worldwide.

Threats to forests

In the past, there were two approaches to logging: clear felling and the selective removal of large timber trees. Even the latter can be environmentally damaging, for example, in Wolong many old hollow trees used by panda mothers as potential den sites were lost. Asiatic black bears also use large hollow trees for hibernation.

Exploitation of bamboo by selectively harvesting from natural bamboo forests can be sustainable, because bamboo is a perennial grass that sends up new shots from the underground rhizomes.

But rapid development of the bamboo industry has intensified the harvest, resulting in over-exploitation that destroys the biodiversity and threatens the animals which feed on bamboo outside panda reserves, including the golden takin and the Chinese bamboo rat.

The diversity of forests is also being reduced by the planting of exotic trees, such as eucalyptus. Planting commercial moso bamboo forests, at Anji (Zhejiang) and

Above far left:
The fragrance of the magnolia *Michelia doltsopa* flowers is often smelt before they become visible.

Above left:
Tree ferns can be seen growing beside the road in Diaoluoshan NRP.

Above top:
A leech crawls along a leaf in Diaoluoshan NRP.

Above:
This clubmoss carpets some areas of the forest floor in Diaoluoshan NRP.

Opposite above:
Leaves of the maidenhair tree (*Ginkgo biloba*) turn pale gold just before they are shed.

Opposite above right:
Feathery leaves of the dawn redwood turn colour prior to leaf fall.

Opposite:
Dove or handkerchief tree flowers have white bracts that flutter in the breeze.

Overleaf left:
Dried fruit of star anise (*Illicium verum*) is a popular spice in Chinese dishes, where it is known as *ba jiao*. It contains essential oils used in the production of the anti-influenza drug Tamiflu.

Overleaf right:
Fruit and leaves of the anti-cancer tree or Chinese happy tree (*Camptotheca acuminata*) contain the anti-cancer drug camptothecin used for treating breast and colon cancer.

Jianyang (Fujian), has created monocultures where there is a huge reduction of plant species beneath the evergreen canopy which allows little light to penetrate.

Impact on any ecosystem comes from high human population pressure and it is not possible to build a large tourist resort – whatever it may be called – without causing damage to the environment, such as the fragmentation of natural green corridors, which are so important for the survival of the giant panda population.

Redressing the balance

The policy of clearing forests for agricultural land during the Great Leap Forward, the Cultural Revolution (1966-76) and the Opening up of Forest Products Markets in the early 1980s was carried out regardless of any thought about providing for sustainable forests in the future or erosion control. This policy is gradually being turned around. Apart from allowing felling for local subsistence, deforestation for agriculture has been banned throughout China since 1998. Nonetheless, small-scale depletion does still occur.

After the disastrous 1998 floods in the Yangtze, Songhua and Nenjiang watersheds, which spread across 29 provinces, the Chinese Government launched the ten-year Grain-for-Green programme in 2000. The aim was to reduce the soil erosion (and hence serious flooding) by farmers planting saplings on sloping farmland in return for cash and grain subsidies. Now over half way through the programme, even though the survival rate of the saplings is only 20-30 per cent, soil erosion is being reduced. Not only is the forest area increasing but also farmers' livelihoods have been improved.

Wanglang NNR is another panda reserve in Sichuan. The knock-on effects of the logging ban here, as elsewhere, is that local people having lost a steady income, turned to illegal logging and the collection of medicinal plants. The WWF is helping to find alternative sources of income including supporting an eco-lodge for small low-impact groups. Outside the reserve are villages were Baima people live and the WWF is helping here too with their sustainable livelihoods project by encouraging bee-keeping, vegetable planting, handicraft production, at the same time promoting ecotourism within the community.

Forests are much more than a collection of trees; they provide a variety of microhabitats which maintain a wealth of biodiversity, halt soil erosion and help flood control. Many forest plants have for long been utilised in traditional medicines,

Above:
Few other plants grow inside a commercial moso bamboo forest at Anji in Anhui where *Crouching Tiger, Hidden Dragon* was filmed.

but now natural chemicals from trees are being identified as having a high biomedical value – for example, anti-cancer drugs. Hence, forests already provide multifarious resources and may well harbour more plants with other life-saving properties that make the conservation of these habitats a top priority.

3

Wetlands

Rivers make their passage across China in different ways: starting as vibrant mountain streams, they may cut through impressive canyons or plunge down spectacular waterfalls before meandering across the plains. Together with lakes and marshlands these wetlands provide essential life-giving elements to the surrounding land.

Here, the lower cascades of Jiulong (Nine Dragons) waterfall in Yunnan have a reduced flow in the dry season.

Rivers

China has a rich assortment of rivers, with most of the larger ones originating from the high Qinghai-Tibetan Plateau (also known as the 'roof of the world'), from where they make a huge descent before spreading out towards the river mouths.

Within the mountains in north Yunnan, three rivers – the Jinsha (which becomes the Yangtze), the Nujiang (also known as the Salween) and the Lancang (the Chinese name for the Mekong, meaning 'turbulent river') run roughly parallel in a north to south direction as they cut through steep gorges. Together, they form the Three Parallel Rivers (Sanjiang Binglui) World Heritage Site, which covers 17,000 square kilometres and is the largest WHS in China. This region is not only the epicentre of Chinese biodiversity, but also one of the world's most biodiverse temperate regions. During the ice ages, it formed a vital north-south corridor for the movement of animals and plants.

On the upper reaches of the Jinsha River is the famous Tiger Leaping (Hutiao) Gorge formed as the river squeezes between Jade Dragon Snow Mountain and Haba Snow Mountain, in a series of rapids. A dam has been proposed on the Jinsha River within the WHS, which could become a reality only if the site boundaries were to be redefined. If the dam was built the dramatic Tiger Leaping Gorge landscape would disappear and many local Naxi people would have to be relocated.

Originating from Tibetan glaciers, the Lancang is the longest river in south-east Asia. It flows south through Yunnan, forming the border between Myanmar and Laos, where it is known as the Mekong. It moves on through Thailand, Cambodia

Opposite:
Sunrise reflected in the Lancang (Mekong) River at Jinghong, Yunnan.

Below:
In winter, snow often falls on the vibrant well-oxygenated upper reaches of the Pitiao River at Wolong NNR in Sichuan.

and Vietnam to the South China Sea. Some 90 million people, in six countries, rely on the river. China has already completed two hydroelectric power stations on the Lancang and with more dams under construction; this threatens the downstream ecosystem in other countries, by changing the natural alternating cycles of flood and drought.

The Mekong giant catfish (*Pangasianodon gigas*), which reaches up to three metres in length, is the largest freshwater fish in the world. A century ago, it used to be found along the Mekong from Vietnam to southern China. Today it occurs only in the lower reaches and is critically endangered.

The Yangtze, Yellow and Pearl rivers all flow east, discharging into the Pacific Ocean. The Yarlung Tsangpo, the biggest river in Tibet AR, starts to flow eastwards, then turns south to empty into the Indian Ocean. As it cuts through the Himalayas it flows through a spectacular 505-kilometre-long canyon, recently confirmed to be the largest in the world. It is also a very lush, green canyon because it forms a moist corridor extending the tropical mountain environment for an extra six degrees northward. Reaching a maximum depth of six kilometres, nine natural vertical climate zones exist within the canyon, ranging from a frigid zone at the top through to a tropical monsoon rainforest zone within the river valley.

The Yellow River or Huang He is China's second largest river and the most silt-laden in the world. Indeed, the name arises from the heavy loess loads, which are picked up as the river flows through the Loess Plateau in the middle reaches and turn the water a yellow ochre colour. The birthplace of the ancient northern Chinese civilizations lay within the basin of this river; however, deposition of sediment loads in the lower reaches has been a persistent problem. Way back in AD 200, levee embankments were built up to confine the river and prevent flooding. But as the riverbed continued to rise the levees were breached causing flood damage, considerable suffering and also loss of life on the flood plain.

Flooding from the Yellow River has resulted in some of the worst natural disasters. During the last 3,000 to 4,000 years, the Yellow River has flooded no fewer than 1,539 times and changed its course 18 times. When the river flooded the North China Plain in 1887, it caused the death of nearly two million people and the 1931 flood was even worse, with almost four million deaths. Such devastation has given rise to the alternative name of 'China's Sorrow' for the river, but now flood control projects are under way.

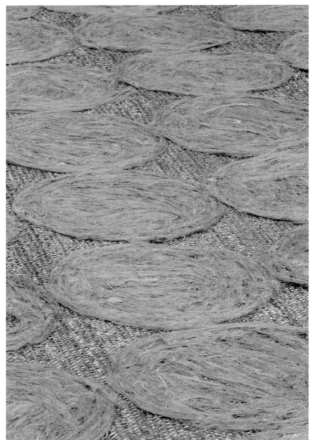

Opposite far left:
Great egrets (*Casmerodius albus*) alighting beside reeds in Yancheng NNR.

Opposite top:
Washing freshwater alga collected from the Lancang (Mekong) River at Menghan in Yunnan. The water is only low enough for the alga to be reached between December and March, so this is a sustainable use of a natural food.

Opposite centre:
A Dai lady arranges freshwater alga collected from the Lancang into a circular mat.

Opposite bottom:
Freshwater algal mats laid out to dry, before frying to eat, Menghan, Yunnan.

Right:
Kanas River flows past a mixed forest in autumn when the birches and larches turn a vibrant gold colour in Kanas NNR, Xinjiang Uygur AR.

Below:
Asian water monitor (*Varanus salvator*) is the largest lizard in China, reaching almost two metres in length. It swims in an S-motion with the limbs pressed against the body.

Overleaf:
Tianchi or Heavenly Lake in Tian Mountains, backed by snow-capped peaks, Xinjiang Uygur AR.

Lakes

Water from streams, rivers, snow and glaciers feed China's lakes. Tibet AR and Qinghai have more lakes than any other part of China; indeed, Tibet's lake statistics are impressive. Over 1,500 lakes – freshwater, saltwater, glacial and barrier – nestle amongst the mountains and plateaux and make up 30 per cent of the total lake area in China. There are many holy lakes in Tibet; Nam Co, which means 'heavenly lake', is the largest fed by snowmelt water and lies at an elevation of 4,740 metres. Pilgrims visit the lake each year, taking 20 to 30 days to walk right round it.

North of Tibet lies the Xinjiang Uygur AR, which is also well endowed with lakes. Close to the Kazakhstan border lies Kanas (Hanasi) Lake NNR at the base of the Altai Mountains. This alpine lake is the widest part of the Kanas River, a tributary of the Ertix River fed by water from the Ertix glacier and bordered by European primaeval forest, Kanas resembles a Scandinavian landscape. The water colour constantly changes; in a single day it may appear an intense blue, turquoise, dark green or grey. Come the autumn, when the birch and larch trees turn a glorious golden colour, the mixed forests are transformed for a brief period. Amongst the fish which thrive in the lake are Manchurian trout (*Brachymystax lenok*) and burbot (*Lota lota*). People flock to Kanas to glimpse a huge fish known as the *huguai* – China's equivalent to the Loch Ness monster, which reputedly is able to swallow a whole duck. Some people think it could be an outsized taimen (*Hucho taimen*), a type of salmon living in deep frigid waters. One over two metres long has been caught in Russia. There are plans to expand Kanas into the largest National Park in China, making it even larger than Yellowstone Park in North America.

Heavenly Lake or Tianchi recurs as a name for Chinese lakes. One of these is a crescent-shaped moraine lake fed by many glaciers within the eastern Tian Mountains. An expressway from Urumqi, a mere 100 kilometres away, makes Tianchi easily accessible – even in winter – when the lake becomes a winter wonderland surrounded by snow-clad mountains. Another lies in a spectacular setting within Changbai Mountains Biosphere Reserve (BR). Originally an active volcano, repeated eruptions have formed a huge crater lake encircled by 16 peaks – nine in China and seven in North Korea. Water from this Tianchi plunges down to form the spectacular 60-metre-high Changbai Grand Waterfall that can be heard from afar.

Bayinbuluk Swan Lake NNR lies at the foot of the Tian Mountains. The lake itself is in essence a series of lakes connected by the zig-zagging Kaidu River, which meanders through grasslands. The lake is so named from the whooper swans (*Cygnus cygnus*) that return here each year to breed.

The largest freshwater lake in China, Poyang Hu, lies on the middle and lower reaches of the Yangtze. This lake is classified as a Ramsar site, which signifies it is a wetland of international importance. The lake level and the area change dramatically with the seasons. The lake is linked to the Yangtze River via a channel that carries floodwater into Poyang Hu. After the April to June flood season, the vast lake begins to shrink to form many small lakes and extensive marshes during the winter and spring dry season.

Copious phytoplankton, together with aquatic plants, feed invertebrates and herbivores that in turn feed a vast number of birds – especially during the mild winter. Small wonder the area attracts international birdwatchers to see a galaxy of cranes (Siberian, white-naped and hooded) and storks (white and black), as well as tundra swans (*Cygnus columbianus*), pied avocets (*Recurvirostra avosetta*), mandarin ducks (*Aix galericulata*) and Dalmatian pelicans (*Pelecanus crispus*).

The prettiest lakes are invariably not the largest and the series that lie within Jiuzhaigou (Nine Village Valley) in Sichuan are quite breathtakingly beautiful. Tucked away in a high mountain valley on the south-west edge of the Qinghai-Tibetan Plateau, known only to the Tibetan villagers who lived there, it was discovered by foresters late in the 1960s. What makes Jiuzhaigou so special is the way lakes are

REBIRTH OF THE YANGTZE

Throughout many dynasties, the Yangtze or Changjiang has been the lifeblood of China's nation; as a means of transport, as a vast resource of natural fish and, by the time it flattens out to form the Yangtze delta, as a huge area for rice cultivation. The life of this mighty river is fed by glacial meltwater on the Geladandong Snowy Mountain in the Qinghai-Tibetan Plateau. It flows south before turning north-east through Chongqing and the Three Gorges until it reaches the East China Sea at Shanghai, 6,300 kilometres later to become Asia's longest river.

Within the upper reaches, which flow from Yubin in Sichuan to Yichang in Hubei, live smaller fish well adapted to surviving tumbling waters. Fish found in the middle reaches stretching from Yichang to Hukou in Jiangxi at the mouth of Poyang Hu, include the curious Chinese sucker (*Myxocyprinus asiaticus*) with sucker-like lips and the Chinese paddlefish (*Psephurus gladius*) with a long cone-shaped rostrum. Both are now threatened by pollution and over-fishing. Together, they shared this stretch of the river with the critically endangered *baiji* or Yangtze river dolphin. When an international research team failed to record a single dolphin after a six-week survey in 2006, chances of rescuing the *baiji* seemed to have been lost, but then a year later, one was seen and recorded on video.

Smaller than the *baiji*, the Yangtze finless porpoise or river pig (*Neophocaena phocaenoides*) has been declining rapidly. Now reserves have been set up to protect this porpoise in Poyang and Dongting Lakes and five animals have been relocated to the cleaner environment of Tian'e-Zhou Semi Natural Baiji Reserve – an isolated oxbow lake originally selected to protect the *baiji*. Since the porpoises were introduced in the 1990's, an average of two calves have been produced each year; however the small genetic diversity could lead to inbreeding.

The lower reaches, which flow from Hukou to the East China Sea, wander through plains as well as large lakes such as Cao Hu and Tai Hu, reaching the sea at Shanghai. Tai Hu is famous for curious eroded limestone rocks – the so-called stones of longevity – much prized in Chinese classical gardens. Many fishes of the lower reaches, which belong to the carp family, are extensively farmed in cages and net enclosures.

Construction of the Three Gorges Dam – the largest hydroelectric river dam in the world – is resulting in many changes to this famous river. Work on the dam began in 1994, but it will not become fully operational before 2011. Benefits gained from the dam will include the control of flooding in the middle and lower reaches, as well as a reduction of greenhouse gases when coal consumption is reduced by 31 million tons per year. However, this massive project involves the relocation of at least 1.4 million residents and the flooding of over 1,000 archaeological sites. So far as wildlife goes, it is the migratory fish which will suffer most because where the dam blocks their passage they are unable to reach their spawning grounds.

Dwindling fish stocks have resulted in a sharp decline in fish catches from 427,000 tons in 1957 to 100,000 tons in recent years. To counteract this falling production and ultimately to produce sustainable fisheries, all fishing is now banned in the upper reaches from 1 February to 30 April and fishing boats are tied up in the middle and lower reaches for three months from 1 April.

The WWF is now working on a wetland restoration programme to restore a living Yangtze, beginning with three lakes in Hubei. Opening the sluice gates that link the Yangtze to Zhangdu Lake and Tain'e-Zhou oxbow has restored the natural seasonal flooding. By restoring reed beds at Hong Hu undrinkable water became drinkable in under a year.

Left:
The Chinese sucker has fat upturned lips. This fish – endemic to China – also migrates up river to spawn and is endangered for the same reasons as the sturgeon. Chinese suckers can weigh up to 30 kilos, but much smaller fish are popular with fish hobbyists.

Opposite:
1. Mudskippers (*Periopthalmus cantonensis*) live in the lower estuarine reaches of the Yangtze.

2. Like many Chinese rivers, the Yangtze has several names along its course. Here, as it flows through an incised meander within the Three Parallel Rivers WHS it is known as the Jinsha (Golden Sand) River.

3. The Chinese three-keeled pond turtle (*Chinemys reevesii*) lives in the upper reaches. Males court females in spring by swimming around them attempting to touch snouts. Over-collection for food and the pet trade has resulted in a sharp decline of this semi-aquatic turtle.

4. Thickets of the endemic *Bauhinia bohniana* grow on slopes above the Jinsha River cutting through the Middle Tiger Leaping Gorge.

5. Carp make up half of the total annual fish catch from the Yangtze. For more than 4,000 years four native species of carp, which live at different depths and feed on different food, have been cultured together. These grass carp (*Ctenopharyngodon idella*) are herbivores, whereas silver and bighead carp both filter feed and black carp crushes crustaceans and clam shells with hardened gill rakers.

6 and 7. The Chinese sturgeon (*Acipenser sinensis*) has an underslung mouth and barbels for feeling along the bottom. This species once reached 400-500 kilos, is now declining in numbers as well as in weight. Endangered by pollution, excessive fishing and obstruction during the upstream migration to spawn, the Chinese Sturgeon Research Institute, set up at Yichang in 1982, has released five million young sturgeon in an attempt to redress the balance.

1

7

6

5

2

3

4

separated by travertine dykes, which have created attractive bifurcating waterfalls. Many of the lakes are a brilliant shade of blue as sunlight is scattered, reflected and absorbed in the water. By 1992, Jiuzhaigou had become a WHS, followed by a Biosphere Reserve in 1997.

Regarded as one of the most beautiful places in China, Jiuzhaigou now attracts 1.5 million visitors a year with hotels capable of taking up to 20,000 a day. Not surprisingly, such mass tourism has a negative impact on this unique and very special location. Even though tourists are transported up the valley in eco-friendly buses, a ring road has fragmented the giant panda's habitat and such an influx of visitors inevitably puts pressure on all wildlife in the area.

South-west of the Yangtze and adjacent to the ancient city of Suzhou, renowned for the abundance of classical gardens, is Yangcheng Lake. Chinese mitten crabs (*Eriocheir sinensis*) used to migrate from the lake towards the Yangtze delta where they mated in September and October. Local fisherman had a bonanza at this time since hairy crabs are considered a great delicacy. Now breeding crabs in the lake is big business and since a more vigorous strain was introduced, few true native crabs exist, so the natural migration no longer takes place. Tiny crabs are bought from northern Jiangsu where they are fattened up within the lake. From October to December they are caught at night and the best quality crabs are exported.

There was a time when the crabs were cursed and considered to be inedible. When Emperor Da Yu sent Bajie 6,000 years ago to supervise the flooding control of the Yangtze, workers along the muddy banks where the crabs burrow complained they kept getting nipped. Bajie ordered a moat to be dug to trap the crabs where they were killed with hot water. The crabs smelt so good he decided to eat one. Having survived, the news quickly spread about these delicious crabs, resulting in Bacheng (Ba town), becoming famous for the crabs, so the town was named after Bajie.

Preceding pages:
Five Flower Lake with autumnal reflections and submerged tree trunks coated with layers of carbonates and bicarbonates (karst) at Jiuzhaigou in Sichuan.

Above:
Arrow Bamboo Lake waterfall in Jiuzhaigou flows over a mix of calcium cement and mosses that form a strong but flexible barrier.

Below:
Floating leaf rosettes of water chestnut (*Trapa natans*) grow on Yangcheng Lake.

Right:
Spiky fruits of water chestnut appear on land as Poyang Hu shrinks in winter. In medieval times, the fruits were scattered on the ground to pierce the hooves of enemy horses.

Below:
The Chinese mitten crab is so-named from the hairy bands that surround the base of each pincer. These crabs are considered a great delicacy in China.

Salt lakes

In north-west China salt lakes abound; indeed there are so many in Qinghai, the Qinghai Institute of Salt Lakes was founded in Xining in 1965. Qinghai Lake is a huge saltwater lake, which resembles an inland sea encircled by mountains. As a sacred lake, pilgrims come to walk around it, taking about 18 days on horseback – much more on foot. Nikolai Przewalski, the Russian explorer, grossly underestimated the time it would take to encircle the lake, reckoning it would be eight days on horseback and 15 on foot. Lying at an altitude of 3,260 metres above sea level, on the Qinghai-Tibetan Plateau, the rich waters attract large numbers of breeding birds in the spring, when the air is thick with wheeling birds, feasting mainly on carp. The naked carp (*Gymnocypris przewalskii*), which is endemic to this lake, is virtually scaleless and considered to be a great delicacy. It migrates back and forth between freshwater rivers where it spawns and the lake where it feeds and grows. Some 100,000 birds including bar-headed geese (*Anser indicus*) and brown-headed gulls (*Larus brunnicephalus*) home in on Egg Island in April and May, but only 9,000 are breeding birds. Great cormorants (*Phalacrocorax carbo*) nest on Cormorant Island. After breeding is over and the birds have left, the lake freezes over for several months.

Decreasing rainfall and underground water supply have resulted in the lake falling 11.7 metres within a century. The pH level has also increased to 9.5 with the result that the average size of fish has decreased and their reproduction rate has fallen.

Salt lakes also occur in Xinjiang Uygur AR; notably Aydingkol Lake which lies 154 metres below sea level in the Turpan Depression – the lowest place in China. As more water was used for agriculture and industrial purposes, less flowed into the lake, which resulted in the water shrinking until it eventually completely dried up in the excessive heat. Salt crystals line the depression, sparkling in the sunlight and glowing in the moonlight.

Hot waters

Geothermal fields exist all over China. Many are used as health spas and some as a source of power. North-west of Lhasa the Yangbajain geothermal station, the first in Tibet AR, was opened in 2000. Near this area there is a huge hot water lake from which steam can rise as high as 100 metres on some days. Also in Tibet AR, Tagegjia, is the largest geyser in China, which rises and falls several times before it blasts skywards for 200 metres. In south-western Tibet AR a reserve has been set up specifically to protect geysers. Covering an area of 400 hectares, it contains geothermal geyser groups that are rare as well as fragile.

Tenchong in west Sichuan is a volcanic hot spot with many dormant volcanoes now clothed with vegetation, but with plenty of active hot springs and geysers. Yihong Hot Lake is one of the biggest hot spring lakes in China and the Bird-Snatching Pool is a vent, which produces a lethal gas mixture of carbon dioxide and hydrogen sulphide that plucks any hapless bird from the sky that happens to fly over it.

Coastal wetlands

Wetlands, which lie inland along the Jiangsu coast, are important staging posts for migrant birds that use them to refuel en route further south, while others remain there during the winter. Despite cold winter winds which can blow inland from the adjacent Yellow Sea, the sheer numbers of wetland birds provide a dramatic spectacle as they wheel in the air. Yet, these areas are threatened by the natural wetlands being converted to fishponds, saltpans and commercial reed beds. Reeds grown for paper production have expanded dramatically in recent years, as have fishponds where the water is too deep for wading birds to feed.

Above:
Red-crowned cranes (*Grus japonicus*) overwinter in Yancheng NNR where they can be seen feeding and flying overhead. This crane is the sole species with white primary feathers.

Opposite:
As the water evaporates, crude salts crystallise at the edge of a salt lake, which is then extracted near Turpan, Xinjiang Uygur AR.

Yancheng NNR (contiguous with Dafeng Milu NNR to the south) is a large reserve, renowned as the world's largest overwintering site for the vulnerable red-crowned crane. These cranes have a varied diet, as they are able to feed in deeper water than other cranes, taking fish, amphibians and aquatic invertebrates. They also feed on insects, reeds and grasses. During the day they can be seen feeding in fields in small groups. As evening approaches, the cranes lift off to fly to their roosting site, producing their haunting calls. Also at Yancheng there is a resident population of Saunders's gulls, which prefer a taste for seafood, feeding on crabs when the tide recedes to expose the mud flats. Amongst the several species of geese that overwinter at Yancheng, are several thousand bean geese (*Anser fabalis*) and greylag geese (*Anser anser*), together with a few hundred swan geese (*Anser cygnoides*).

Above:
Père David's deer hind, feed with attendant cattle egrets at Dafeng Milu NNR, Jiangsu.

Opposite above:
Swamp foxtail grass in flower at Dafeng Milu NNR.

Opposite below:
A Père David's deer stag stands in a sward of flowering swamp foxtail grass at Dafeng Milu NNR, Jiangsu.

Overleaf:
A colourful dawn sky becomes reflected in the myriad pools separated by curvaceous lines within the 1,300-year-old rice terraces at Yuanyang in Yunnan.

Back from the brink

Several endangered animals that live associated with wetlands have been brought back from the brink of extinction by means of captive breeding. Notably 20 Père David's deer or *milu* (see p8) were reintroduced in 1984 to Nan Haizi (now known as Beijing Milu Park), the location where they were last kept in China. A year later, 39 deer were reintroduced to Dafeng Milu NNR on the banks of the Yangtze, in Jiangsu. Fossil *milu* have been found in nearly 200 locations, 127 of them in Jiangsu, which proves the Yangtze delta was the preferred habitat for the ancestral *milu*. The reintroduced deer, all descendents from a small group transported from China to Europe, have adapted well to the humid warm subtropical climate in central eastern China.

In Dafeng, many are kept in large enclosures while others have been released and some have escaped into the natural habitat. The deer are well adapted to walking through marshy ground with their broad splayed-out feet, feeding on the new shoots of swamp foxtail grass (*Pennisetum aloperuroides*). In winter they feed on the roots of this and other grasses, when they are also fed with supplementary food. It is a common sight at Dafeng to see cattle egrets in attendance with the deer, on the ground or perched on their backs, ready to swoop on insects disturbed by the trampling hooves. The herd has increased steadily in this coastal marshland strip, reaching 1,169 head in 2007. A *milu*-watching pavilion completed at Dafeng in 2004 is a replica of the one built in 1767 by order of Emperor Qianlong at Nan Haizi.

Tian'e-Zhou in central Hubei was selected as the third major location for introducing Père David's deer – 30 in 1993 and 34 a year later – because the habitat is very similar to the central and lower Yangtze basin which was their natural home. Researchers at Tian'e-Zhou are surprised how the *milu* have reproduced through many generations without showing signs of negative aspects attributed to inbreeding. It is possible that competition during the rutting season when the deer mate helps to ensure the strongest genes are passed on.

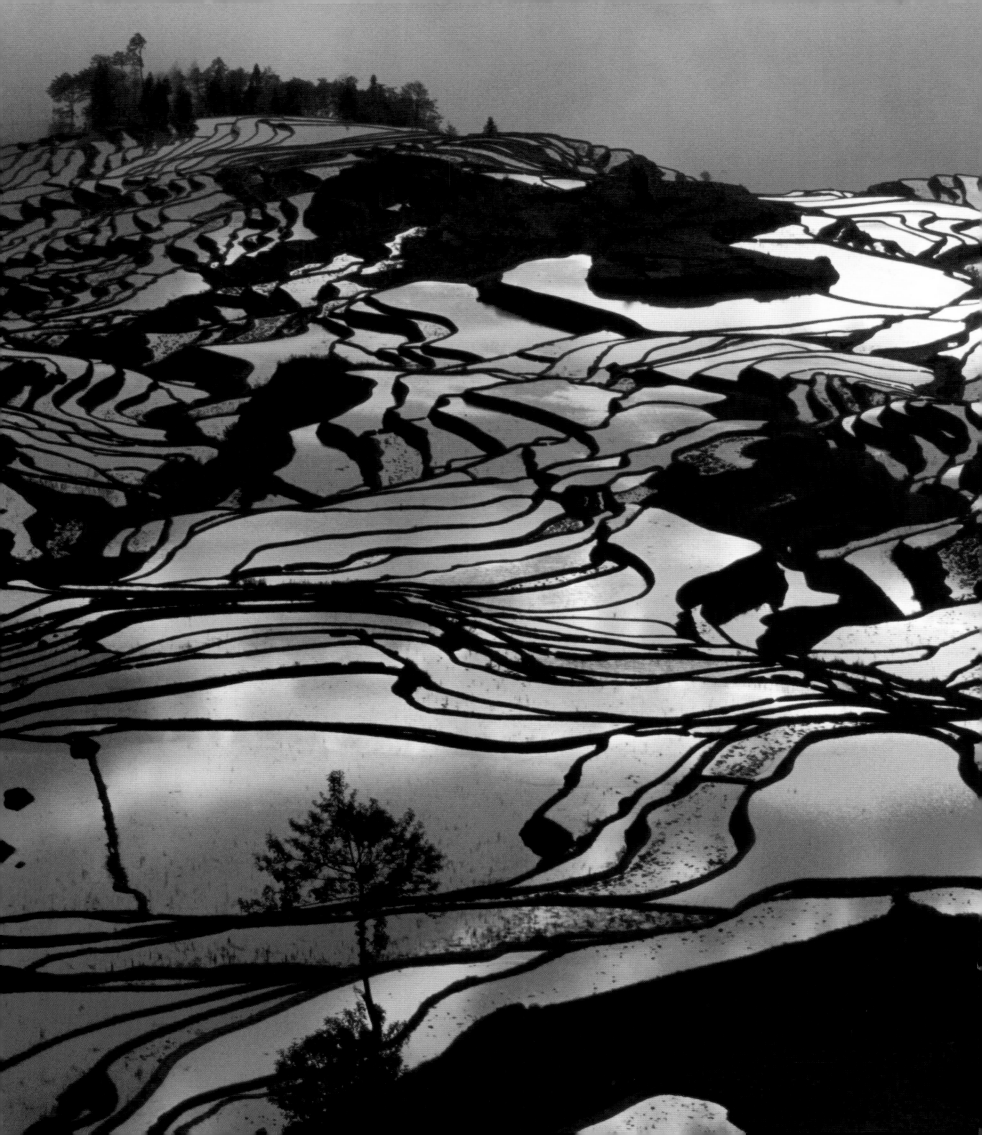

The striking crested ibis (*Nipponia nippon*) with a pink body, vermilion face, a long curving bill, bushy crest and crimson legs was once widespread in north-east Asia up until the end of the nineteenth century. But loss of natural wetlands to agriculture, logging of nesting trees and use of pesticides has resulted in the numbers plummeting until the ibis was thought to have become extinct in the wild. That was until 1981 when seven birds (four adults and three chicks) were discovered in Yang Xian county in Shaanxi, to the west of the central Chinese wetlands area. After logging ceased and agrochemicals were banned, this sole wild population has increased steadily to some 360 birds. Farmers who no longer use fertilisers and pesticides are compensated.

Captive breeding programmes have been set up in Yang Xian County and at Beijing Zoo and in an attempt to preserve the genetic diversity, one ibis is transferred from the wild to Beijing each year, since animals bred from a small gene pool tend to be less able to cope with diseases or climatic extremes.

Foraging in rice fields and along riverbanks, the crested ibis feeds on frogs, newts, crabs, small fish and freshwater molluscs. Even though a Crested Ibis Conservation and Observation Station has been set up in Shaanxi, some birds are still lost from illegal hunting and by feeding on poisoned baits. Also, the draining of rice fields for wheat production has reduced the winter-feeding grounds; and after dead birds were found to have empty stomachs, some of the fields are now stocked with loach as winter food for the ibis.

The two-metre long Chinese or Yangtze alligator used to frequent the lower Yangtze living in slow-moving rivers, streams and swamps. Known locally as *tu long* or 'muddy dragon' it is just half the size of the American alligator. Draining the

Above:
The totally aquatic Chinese giant salamander has a huge head with a wide gape and lateral skin folds increase the area for oxygen absorption. It has small eyes and hunts at night, feeding on freshwater shrimps and crabs, as well as frogs and fish.

Below:
With the natural wetland habitat of the Chinese alligator being converted to rice fields, this top predator is now nearing extinction in the wild. A captive breeding programme is now under way for this reptile, known locally as muddy dragon.

Above:
The aquatic fern (*Azolla*) and duckweed often carpet rice paddies in winter.

Below:
The oriental fire-bellied toad (*Bombina orientalis*) lives in mountain lakes and ponds. When threatened, it arches up the body to reveal the warning colours beneath the green back.

Below right:
The attractive Chinese fire-bellied newt (*Cynops orientalis*) is threatened by collection, from cold mountain ponds and rice terraces, for the pet trade.

marshland for agricultural land and dam building brought about a rapid decline of this alligator until it became critically endangered, with a wild population of less than 200 animals. It feeds between April and October on freshwater snails and mussels, which are crushed with powerful teeth. Between July and August, alligators build a nest mound of plant debris inside which the eggs are laid. Young alligators take around 70 days to develop, and like other species, sex of the hatchings is determined by incubation temperature, with males being produced at higher temperatures (above 33°C). Half of the year is spent hibernating in elaborate underground burrows in which the temperature stays around 10°C.

In 1979 the Anhui Chinese Alligator NNR was set up and a captive breeding programme initiated. Since the first hatching in 1988, the breeding rate has proved to be very successful with a single alligator capable of producing up to 50 eggs; over 10,000 alligators have hatched out. Since 2003, scientists have released 15 captive-bred Chinese alligators on three separate occasions in Anhui.

Within cool, highly oxygenated mountain streams in north, central and south China lives the largest amphibian in the world. Although endangered and protected, the Chinese giant salamander, which can grow up to 150 cm in length, is still hunted for food in some areas. After collection from Sijian Mountain in Guangxi Zhuang AR was forbidden in 2000, the giant salamander began to appear again and here a giant salamander reserve was set up. Key objectives within a 10-year plan include provision of essential breeding sites lost by dam construction, as well as a captive breeding programme. Giant salamanders have an unusual breeding behaviour whereby a den site, such as a cave, is occupied by a male who supervises the breeding and development. He appears to take no part in the reproduction but allows both females and other males into the den. After spawning he, as den master, guards the den and protects the eggs.

Cultivated wetlands

Throughout most of the country, rice fields and terraces together contribute a huge temporary wetland environment for many months of the year. Here, frogs, aquatic insects and the aquatic ferns, Azolla and Marsilea, flourish. Although rice is the staple food in China, the total growing area has declined during the last quarter century as farmers have diversified their crops. The total area devoted to rice growing in China has dropped from 370,000 square kilometres in the mid-1970s to around 300,000 square kilometres today. Rice fields in the Yangzte basin provide vital feeding grounds

Left:
Inside the lotus lily flower the stamens surround a flat receptacle in which the seeds are embedded.

Below:
Aquatic plants in Napa Hai, a seasonal lake near Zhongdian in Yunnan, which swells when the snow melts from the surrounding mountains.

Opposite:
The Chinese water dragon (*Physignathus cocincinus*) lives in southern China and although it is a popular pet it is not yet endangered. This lizard can climb trees and swim. When not hunting frogs, fish and insects, it is often found hauled out on river banks or lounging on tree trunks.

for many larger overwintering birds, which can wade out to feed. Many rice paddies in Hubei and Hunan were converted to cotton fields and lotus ponds in the 1990s, resulting in the decline of wintering hooded cranes.

China recognises that wetlands are a vastly important ecosystem both for wildlife and as a natural resource; but they can only be maintained if they are managed in a sustainable way. In particular, the unique Yangtze wetlands have a rich assortment of wildlife, some of which came perilously close to extinction. But in recent years, steps have been taken to help restore this internationally important wetland area. Since 2001, the WWF has implemented the Wetland Ambassadors Campaign, which helps university students with funding and training for wetland projects. In 2005, the Yangtze Forum brought together key people – both provincial governors and ministers – who signed the Yangtze Declaration to sustainably develop the Yangtze basin.

Lotus is planted as an aquatic crop either on its own or mixed with arrowroot (*Sagittaria sagittifolia*). The time of planting lotus roots or rhizomes varies with latitude; in south China it is in late March, in central China in the first part of April, while in north China it is not planted until May or June.

The lotus root is a nutritious food and when sectioned into slices the large air chambers are visible. The lotus root is dug from the soil between July and October, depending on the region. Lotus seeds are also eaten but, like the plants grown for their attractive flowers, have to be grown separately. Sweet and crispy lotus seeds are gathered by hand to be sundried before being eaten as a summer treat.

Lotus ponds are often rotated with fish culture, but in some cases they are cultivated together in the same pond. As the lotus plants grow, the water level is increased and tilapia added when it is 30 centimetres deep. The fish can feed on epiphytic algae that grow on the lotus shoots. As a sacred plant, lotus is widely grown adjacent to Buddhist temples.

Arrowroot is an aquatic perennial, which has been farmed in the Yangtze area since Neolithic times. It is distinguished from lotus by the distinct arrow-shaped leaves. The tubers are boiled, steamed or baked and eaten like potatoes. The Chinese water chestnut (*Eleocharis dulcis*) is another aquatic grown in rotation with other crops including rice, for their corms that are either eaten fresh or cooked in stir-fry dishes. It also produces a starch used for thickening sauces. This plant should not be confused with the water chestnut illustrated on pages 74 and 75 which is cultivated for its fruit that is eaten raw or cooked. Flour obtained from the seeds is used medicinally and for making wine.

WINTER VISITORS

Many birds which breed in high northern latitudes that become frozen in winter migrate south to warmer winter feeding grounds. China's central east coast is an important stopover for birds to refuel as they migrate south on the East Asian Flyway. Many more remain in China as their winter resort and notable places where vast numbers of wetland birds congregate are Poyang Hu NNR and Yancheng NNR.

Poyang Hu in Jiangxi is a globally important wetland reserve for both the range of species found there in winter as well as the sheer numbers of some endangered birds. During the summer rainy season, this shallow lake with an average depth of only eight metres, becomes China's largest lake extending to 5,500 square kilometres, as it swells from overflow from the Yangtze River. It gradually fragments into a series of shallow winter lakes which form ideal feeding grounds for many wildfowl.

It is here that 95 per cent (4,000 birds) of the total world population of the endangered Siberian crane (*Grus leucogeranus*) can be found in winter. As the water level in Poyang Hu drops, these large white cranes feed on exposed roots and tubers. White-naped cranes (*Grus vipio*) migrate from eastern Mongolia, southern Siberia and north China to Poyang Hu and other lakes in the lower Yangtze basin to feed on cultivated lands. Hooded cranes (*Grus monacha*), which breed in north Siberia and north-east China, are much rarer at Poyang Hu; many more overwinter in south Japan.

Sharing Poyang Hu's winter quarters with the cranes are thousands of tundra swans, greater white-fronted geese (*Anser albifrons*), swan geese, tundra bean geese (*Anser serrirostris*) plus many oriental storks (*Ciconia boyciana*) and pied avocets which breed in north China.

Yancheng NNR which lies along the Yellow Sea coast, is a mix of coastal grasslands, reed beds, shrimp ponds and saltpans. Here some of the red-crowned cranes which breed in Zhalong NR in Heilongjiang and in south-east Siberia come to overwinter. To protect a breeding site over the border in Russian Far East, Muraviovka Park – the first private nature reserve in all Russia – was set up on lowlands beside the Amur River. This crane, also known as the Japanese crane, is Japan's national bird and a distinct population remains year-round on the island of Hokkaido.

Black-necked cranes (*Grus nigricollis*) breed in high altitude freshwater wetlands on much of the Qinghai-Tibetan Plateau in Qinghai. They migrate to six overwintering areas in north-east Yunnan, west Guizhou and south central Tibet AR. As with all cranes, this species is threatened by loss or change of habitat. For example, after Cao Hai Lake in Guizhou was drained in 1975, the crane numbers dropped to 35. Then, after the lake was restored in the 1980s, gradually more cranes returned until 400 appeared in 1994. An active conservation programme is now underway here. Black-necked cranes tolerate the presence of local people and often feed close to livestock and settlements. During breeding, they

feed on plant roots and tubers, snails, shrimps and small fish. In the winter they feed on waste grain and other remains in cultivated fields but they have been known to damage winter crops – such as potatoes and carrots. Hunting of black-necked cranes is now banned in China, India and Bhutan. Much larger numbers of bar-headed geese (*Anser indicus*) come to overwinter in central China, often feeding alongside the black-headed cranes.

Whooper swans from Sanjiang NNR in Heilongjiang and from Swan Lake in Xining begin to fly south in October to several bays around the north-east coast of Shandong. Most swans overwinter here in Rongcheng Swan NR – notably in Swan Lake – from mid-November to March. According to Yuan Xue Shun, Director of Weihai Swan Protection Association who has been observing the winter visitors for three decades, the number of swans returning to Rongcheng has fluctuated over the years. In 1992, more than 6,000 arrived, but after one overwintering lake was lost to agriculture only 400 swans returned in 1993. Some birds are injured or killed when they get caught in traps or fishing lines or they fly into overhead power lines on foggy days; but by 2007, the numbers had increased to 2,600 swans.

Left:
Bar-headed geese feeding in a turnip field at Daqiao, Yunnan.

Opposite:
1. Whooper swans at dusk in Rongcheng Swan NR in winter.

2. A hooded crane lowers its feet and calls prior to landing.

3. Coming into land, an elegant red-crowned crane shows its distinctive red crown and striking black and white plumage.

4. A group of hooded cranes fly overhead at dusk.

5. Bar-headed geese in flight in Yunnan in winter.

1

2

3

4

5

Deserts and Grasslands

Within the deserts – which extend over a vast part of north-west China – the greatest temperature extremes of any ecosystem occur. These harsh environments may experience soaring heat by day and plummeting temperatures at night. Together with grasslands, they cover virtually half of the country north-west of a rough diagonal line from Tibet AR up to the north-east of Inner Mongolia AR.

As the Murtuk River flows through the Flaming Mountains it transforms the desert in the Turpan Depression into a green ribbon of life.

By no means all deserts (*shamo* in Chinese) are sandy; they may be stony or even covered in bare rock. Unlike rainforests, which are highly biodiverse habitats, only a limited range of species are able to exist in deserts and these have special adaptations for conserving precious water. In the past, many travellers crossing the deserts became disorientated and failed to find a way out; but after oil was discovered beneath the deserts, good access roads were built to reach the oilfields, which have made some parts much more accessible.

Deserts, perhaps more than any other environment, can undergo dramatic changes as a result of changing weather. Today, the Badain Jaran Desert in the western part of the Inner Mongolia AR is a source of major sandstorms; but cultural sites dating from the Paleolithic Age to the Shang and Zhou Dynasties, unearthed by archaeologists in recent years, prove this region was once a paradise for both animals and people.

Some 4,000-7,000 years ago, oases developed after many lakes appeared in the desert. Ruins beside these lakes, together with recently discovered Neolithic and Bronze Age rock paintings depicting herding and hunting scenes, camels, horses, deer and argali, are proof of ancient settlements. Climate change 3,000 years ago brought about the demise of the Badain Jaran civilisation: as it became cold and dry, so the lakes dried up and the desert expanded.

Desert types

Asia's largest desert – the Gobi – covers southern Mongolia and much of northern China. It lies on a plateau averaging 910-1,520 metres in altitude covering an area of 1,295,000 square kilometres, making it the fourth largest desert in the world. Much of the area is bare rock together with stony 'gobi' desert plains, flat pavements, washed plains and sand dunes. The Gobi is so dry because rain-bearing clouds from the west are checked by the Himalayas to create a rain shadow area over the desert.

High latitude and altitude make it a cold desert with frost and even some snow dusting the sand dunes in winter. Snow blowing over the desert from the Siberian Steppes adds a little moisture to the scanty 194 millimetres summer rainfall. The summer searing temperatures reach over 50ºC, only to plummet to -40ºC in winter when icy sandstorms whip across the desert.

In spite of the harsh environment, drought-resistant shrubs such as saltworts, saltbushes and ground-hugging grasses exist here together with specially adapted insects, reptiles, birds and mammals. Traditional palm-fringed oases of the hotter African deserts are replaced here by Euphrates poplar (*Populus euphratica*). The resident wildlife include Asiatic wild ass (*Equus hemionus*), argali – a type of sheep – (*Ovis ammon*) and the wild Bactrian camel (*Camelus bactrianus ferus*); while snow leopards and wolves make occasional visits.

The largest population of the Asiatic wild ass is found mainly in southern Mongolia, where huge herds up to 1,200 animals occur, with some overflowing into China's northern provinces. The ass has a similar fawn body colouration and a dark mane as the Przewalski's horse (*Equus ferus przewalskii*), but has a more slender build, with a less bushy tail. During the summer, wild asses never stray further than 15 kilometres from water; whereas in winter they can disperse further afield eating snow as a source of water. In arid parts of Mongolia, they have been known to dig holes down half a metre in dry river beds to reach water.

Turpan (*Turfan*) and Dunghuang are oasis towns in the Gobi, where underground cool rooms and shade cast by vine-covered terraces make the scorching summer heat bearable. Turpan is famous for melon and grape crops, which are irrigated using an ancient underground *karez* system of water channels. These date back to 103 BC and carry snowmelt water to the fertile land. The *karez* are made by digging lines of vertical shafts linked by tunnels along which precious water flows beneath the scorching desert.

Above:
Bactrian or two hump camel in desert, Xinjiang Uygur AR.

Opposite above:
Edible fruits of *Elaeagnus angustifolia* are known as desert dates, in Xinjiang Uygur AR.

Opposite centre:
Cryptic lizard pauses on desert sand near Turpan, Xinjiang Uygur AR.

Opposite below:
Cracked desert surface near the Flaming Mountains in the Turpan Depression.

Right:
Euphrates or huyang poplar grows with tamarisk (*Tamarix* sp.) along the Tarim River in Luntai County.

To the west of the Gobi region is the vast Tarim basin, which together with Lop Nor and Hami (*Kumul*) basin form China's driest and warmest desert – the Taklamakan. Here, 85 per cent of the crescent-shaped dunes have little or no vegetation cover and the dust storms are so severe they can be seen from space. The Taklamakan is the world's largest shifting sand desert, through which the Tarim River flows from west to east, creating poplar-fringed oases in places. This braided river carries a lot of sand and constantly changes course; local people refer to it as an 'unharnessed wild horse'. Shrinking glaciers and water extraction for irrigation have reduced the flow in recent years. The shifting sand makes this desert inhospitable for humans, so that the wildlife is less threatened than other deserts and small populations of wild Bactrian camels and Asian wild asses still occur there. The dry air of the Taklamakan Desert helps to preserve ancient artefacts; a pair of 2,000-year-old

mummies discovered in the 1990s were still wearing their silk clothing dating back to the Han Dynasty.

Until the middle of the last century, a tiger used to stalk its prey through reeds and gallery forest that flourished alongside the Tarim River and Lop Nor Lake. This was the so-called Tarim tiger (*Panthera tigris lecoqi*). But when water was extracted for irrigation, the lake dried up and the tiger lost both its cover and accessible prey; it was further threatened as more people moved into the area. Known elsewhere as the Caspian tiger, (*Panthera tigris virgata*) it once roamed through countries from Iran, through Afghanistan, Turkey and Mongolia.

The Lop Nor Desert on the eastern edge of the Taklamakan extends eastwards from Korla to the Tarim basin. During spring, fierce sandstorms blast and erode the desert, creating two to six-metre-deep parallel gullies carrying the particles that build up gigantic sand dunes on the edge of the Taklamakan desert. Piles of freshwater mollusc shells (*Planorbis* and *Limnaea* spp.) together with dead tamarisks and Euphrates poplars, as well as withered reed beds on top of *yardangs* – sharp edged ridges of sand – are proof that extensive freshwater lakes once covered this area.

In 2000, the Lop Nor Wild Camel NR in the south-east of Xinjiang Uygur AR, was designated to protect the highly endangered wild Bactrian camel, but the argali and Tibetan wild ass (*Equus kiang*) also benefit. The two humps of the Bactrian camel store fat and when it is well fed and watered both humps are firm. A camel can survive for nine days without water and for a month without food. In winter, they eat snow to maintain their fluid levels. Wild camels are much leaner and taller than domesticated camels, which have been bred for thousands of years. The extra long eyelashes of the Bactrian camel help to protect the eyes during sand storms, when the nostrils can close. These camels feed on saltbushes, saxaul (*Haloxylon ammodendron*), and Euphrates poplar. Surveys undertaken by expeditions in 1995 and 1996, within the Xinjiang Uygur AR and Gansu, estimate the total number of wild camels left to be just 380–500 individuals, which means there are now much fewer camels than there are giant pandas in the wild. Young camels that do not adapt to drinking salt water in Gashun Gobi Desert perish; others may fall prey to wolves.

In north-west China, north of the Tian Mountains, lies the Junggar basin. Cooler than Taklamakan it has more rainfall and so more extensive vegetation. This large area of semi-desert is one of the last places where wild Przewalski's horses are known

Above:
A wolf rests on a grassy knoll in the desert.

Above left:
Grapes hung in a well-ventilated grape house take 30 days to form sultanas, near the Flaming Mountains.

Above centre:
Exhibit shows how a man was lowered and raised into a vertical shaft of the *karez* irrigation system, which dates back to the Han Dynasty in Turpan.

-

Above:
Saxaul flowers, with pendulous sappy branches that function like leaves.

Above right:
A large saxaul tree in flower at Ghost City north-east of the oil town Karamay. This is an important plant used in the restoration of deserts in China.

Below:
Long branches covered with small pink tamarisk flowers enliven the desert, attracting insects such as this hoverfly (*Eristalis* sp.).

to have existed before they became extinct in the wild in the 1960s. The Przewalski's Horse Reintroduction Project was initiated in 1985 and the first group of 55 wild horses was released into the Kalamely Mountain area in Xinjiang Uygur AR where their ancestors once roamed.

Once widespread across Central Asia, over a million saiga antelopes (*Saiga tatarica*) roamed over Kazakhstan and Russia as recently as 1993. Around this time, in an effort to save the rhino, conservationists encouraged male saiga horn to be used in TCM as a cure for fevers as an alternative to rhino horn. Wild saiga become extinct in China in the 1960s, so hunters in Russia and Kazakhstan, using motorcycles and high-powered weapons, began the slaughter of male saiga for their horns to export. Within a decade, the saiga population had plummeted by 97 per cent, leaving mostly females. Between 1988 and 1991, eight saiga were transferred from zoos in Germany and the United States to the Gansu Endangered Wildlife Breeding Centre, where they are being bred for release back into the wild. By 2007, this captive-bred herd totalled 52 animals.

The most plentiful desert mammals are gerbils and jerboas. The latter are distinguished by their extra long hind legs, used for making impressive bounds across the desert. Gerbils, in common with many rodents, can breed very rapidly producing several litters a year resulting in huge population explosions. When giant gerbil (*Rhombomys opimus*) populations explode, their burrowing contributes to erosion and desertification of the north-western Xinjiang Uygur AR.

Reptiles are generally better adapted to desert life than warm-blooded mammals; lizards are the most abundant desert reptiles. During sandstorms they protect their eyes by closing their eyelids. Geckos, on the other hand, have no eyelids and emerge at night to feed on insects when winds tend to die down. Other desert reptiles include snakes and just one kind of tortoise, Horsdfield's tortoise (*Testudo horsfieldi*), which lives in north-west Xinjiang Uygur AR feeding on desert plants.

At high altitude on the Tibetan Plateau are even colder alpine deserts. Hard frosts occur all year round almost every night; sub-zero temperatures, which persist for 9-10 months of the year, create permafrost. To the east of this region, at an altitude of 4,200 metres, lies one of China's largest nature reserves. Arjin Shan NNR is an extensive steppe desert supporting many rare Tibetan animals including wild yak (*Bos grunniens*), Asiatic wild ass, Tibetan wild ass, Tibetan antelope (*Pantholops hodgsonii*), blue sheep (*Pseudois nayaur*) and Tibetan gazelle.

Threats to deserts

As deserts become more accessible with new access roads, they are being degraded in many ways. Trampling of vegetation, whether by livestock or off-road vehicles, damages the already sparse vegetation. Inflated prices for cashmere wool have encouraged an increase in the goat population which overgraze both desert and grassland habitats. Pumping up water from boreholes has lowered the ground water level, as well as boosted the livestock concentrations, which leads to over-grazing.

Farmers have been translocated from other parts of China to both the Taklamakan and the Qaidam Basin to the east. Increased extraction of water for irrigation threatens the desert oases. In the Tarim Basin, the gene pool of wild camels could be threatened if they were to breed with domesticated camels which occur in the area. However, if it could be proved that the Chinese and Mongolian wild camel populations had interbred in recent historic times, the gene flow could be encouraged between these two populations.

In the northern part of Lop Nor NNR, illegal miners use land mines at waterholes to kill Bactrian camels for food. Within the Great Gobi Desert, potassium cyanide used in illegal gold mining poisons plants and animals. The hunting of wild camels has been prohibited since 1930 but habitat loss and pollution have contributed to their critically endangered status. Simple ways in which these vulnerable animals can be aided include the provision of more drinking points and the education of local communities. Even though hunting of wild asses has been banned since 1953, they still suffer from illegal hunting both for their meat and their skins as well as from habitat degradation.

Desertification and the Great Green Wall

Mobile sand dunes are naturally driven forward by persistent winds, and past settlements around the edges of China's deserts have been engulfed by sand. Overgrazing, deforestation, overuse of natural water resources, drought and global warming have all contributed to more rapid desertification. The southern edge of the Gobi is encroaching onto grassland at a rate of 3,600 square kilometres per year. This process of desertification results in loss of grazing land as well as more frequent dust storms.

Minqin, an oasis town in Gansu, began to be engulfed by deserts advancing on two sides – the Badain Jaran from the north and the Tengger from the east – in the 1950s and the 1960s and desertification is now accelerating along the oasis towns in the Hexi Corridor. Over the last 2,000 years, some 38 ancient cities had to be abandoned in this area because of the encroaching desert. At Minqin Desert Botanical Garden, research is being done into ways of slowing down the advance of the desert sand. This was the first place to use soil on the sand to stabilise it. Another experimental approach is to set up one-metre-square checkerboard plots with either green plastic mesh strips or lines of wheat straw to check the blowing sand, but it may not be enough to save Minqin from the marching deserts. The Shapotou Desert Experimental Research Station at the southern end of the dunes on the banks of the Yellow River in Ningxia Hui AR, is also researching dune stabilisation using grasses and microbial mats. Areas, which were stabilised in the 1950s, are now producing fruits and grapes.

China is undertaking one of the most ambitious ecological projects ever attempted. Every spring, dust from the deserts is carried by winds blowing eastwards to Beijing with the result that the capital is coated with desert dust. The dunes are

Above:
Male and female saiga antelopes in the herd at Gansu Endangered Wildlife Breeding Centre.

Opposite above left:
Ephedra forms dense tufts of slender jointed stems. They contain ephedrine, which acts like adrenaline, and has been used for TCM for more than 2,000 years.

Opposite top:
The Mongolian gerbil (*Meriones unguiculatus*) is a desert rodent, which eats roots and seeds. It is a popular pet the world over.

Opposite centre:
Calligonum fruits at Turpan Desert Botanical Garden. This desert plant is used for wind and sand protection.

Opposite bottom:
A lizard in the process of shedding its skin in the Gansu desert.

Right:
Wheat straw checkerboard used to check moving sand growing with Euphrates poplar, Xinjiang Uygur AR.

now within 75 kilometres of China's capital and within 48 kilometres of Shenyang, a city in Liaoning with 7.2 million people. To counteract the advancing dunes, 4,480 kilometres of forest belts will be planted over a period of 70 years, with the aim of providing a windbreak to hold back the advancing desert. Launched in 1978 and

Left:
Goitered gazelles (*Gazella subgutturosa*) are agile fast runners over the desert, where they seasonally migrate.

Below top:
A whooper swan wades out to drink.

Below centre:
Swards of primulas (*Primula secundiflora*) and buttercups enliven the wetter grassland areas at Napa Hai NR in June.

Bottom:
Euphorbia clumps untouched by stock, are a feature of grasslands in the Zhongdian region, Yunnan.

known as the Great Green Wall, more than nine million acres of forest will be planted using both aerial seeding on less arid soil and hand planting of trees and shrubs by farmers. By 2010, green forest belts will extend from outside Beijing into Inner Mongolia AR along the edge of the Gobi Desert. Sceptics doubt the arid desert will be able to support the trees for them to be an effective barrier and that they will extract valuable moisture from the desert.

Grasslands

China's grasslands cover 40 per cent of the country with more than half in the north of the country, notably the dry steppes on the Tibetan Plateau; and the wetter grasslands, with longer grasses, in the north-east. Throughout northern China, most precipitation falls in the summer growing season, winters are very cold and, apart from snowstorms, dry.

Grasslands are not always pure habitats; often they merge with other vegetation. Notably, they intermingle with deserts as the substrate and the water retention varies. This also affects tree growth in mountains where alpine pastures persist on soils that are too thin to support coniferous forests. Wetlands and grasslands co-exist where there are lakes or rivers, sometimes creating a grassland/wetland mosaic.

Napa Hai Nature Reserve is a good example of how a habitat can oscillate between being a grassland or a wetland according to the season. Lying at an altitude of 3,260 metres near Zhongdian (now being marketed to tourists as Shangri La) in Yunnan, it contains a seasonal lake, which floods during the summer when the snow melts in the surrounding mountains. As the water shrinks the area becomes extensive grassland that is grazed by horses, dzos (a male hybrid of a yak and a cow), sheep and pigs. Endangered black-necked cranes come here to overwinter and are becoming a tourist attraction, although the numbers of birds are declining slightly each year.

The extensive Qinghai-Tibetan Plateau has high cold meadows and steppe in the east and south and high cold semi-desert and desert in the north and west. The Tibetan Steppe, which includes grasslands in Tibet AR, Qinghai, west Sichuan, north-west Yunnan and west Gansu, is one of the most important and highest grasslands in the world. Much lies above 4,000 metres where some 12 million yak and 30 million sheep and goats are kept.

The WWF include the Tibetan Steppe in their list of 200 ecoregions with rich biodiversity areas that need priority for conservation. Annual precipitation varies from 600 millimetres in the east to less than 60 millimetres in the west where much

Above:
Napa Hai NR near Zhongdian in Yunnan in summer when it becomes a vast grassland area, with streams zig-zagging through it.

falls as wet snow or hail during June to September. Western grasslands are exposed to strong winds for up to a third of the year. Many of the plants that grow on the plateau are endemic as are several ungulates, which graze on them, including Tibetan wild ass, wild yak, Tibetan antelope and Tibetan gazelle. Predatory birds include the steppe eagle (*Aquila nipalensis*), upland buzzard (*Buteo hemilasius*) and saker falcon (*Falco cherrug*). Snow finches (*Montifringilla* spp.) and pheasants are ground-living birds, which occur at high elevations.

After the severe winter, birds such as black-necked cranes return to nest in the high altitude grassy marshlands, where they forage in shallow marshes and pastures. Bayanbulak Grassland at the south-east foot of Tian Mountains in Xinjiang Uygur AR is an extensive grassland where whooper swans breed with little more than grazing sheep and cattle and the odd yurt as neighbours. Swan Lake, where they congregate, is a vast marshland filled with numerous connected small lakes and reedy marshes that are fed by springs and streams. Bayanbulak, the second largest grassland in China, is home to Mongol, Tibetan and six other ethnic groups who contribute to the area's cultural diversity. Each year around June, the Nadam Fair is held at Bayanbulak.

The Bashang Grassland is the nearest prairie to Beijing in Hebei at the junction of the North China Plain and the Inner Mongolia Plateau. In summer when the weather is cool, many visitors converge here to escape the Beijing heat and to enjoy the wildflowers; in winter, the area is covered with snow.

High-altitude grassland occurs in valleys and on mountain slopes from 3,500-4,500 metres in south-west Gansu, west Sichuan, south-east and east Qinghai, north-west Yunnan and into Tibet AR up to Lhasa, makes up 45 per cent of all China's grasslands. An array of choice alpines grows amongst the grasses, including anemones, louseworts, androsaces, gentians and primulas. At the Haibei Research Station, 160 kilometres north of Xining, there is an example of an alpine meadow ecosystem at 3,200 metres elevation. Here, the Chinese zokor (*Myospalax fontanierii*) a medium-sized rodent that uses outsized claws on the front limbs for digging, contributes to grassland degradation by overgrazing and burrowing.

Many Kazakhs have moved over the border into the north-west of Xinjiang Uygur AR, and here Kazakh hunters continue to train golden eagles (*Aquila chrysaetos*) to hunt rabbits and marmots. But it is corsac foxes (*Vulpes corsac*) they prize most of all for their pelts used to line hats and coats for the severe winters. Early winter is the best time for hunting when the foxes have their winter pelts. The art of successful hunting relies on perfect coordination between the hunter, his horse and the eagle. Kazakh hunters in the Altai region of Xinjiang Uygur AR stop hunting on 20 February, to allow female corsac foxes to breed, and after a decade of hunting, captured eagles are freed so they can find a wild mate and breed.

With the Altai region being developed for ecotourism, the Chinese Government have been reinforcing the hunting ban by fining hunters, confiscating furs and releasing eagles into the wild. Although the corsac fox is declining here, it is not regionally endangered, whereas the golden eagle is endangered in both China and Kazakhstan.

Right:
The corsac fox is hunted in winter by eagles trained by Kazakh herdsmen.

Below:
Golden eagles are used for hunting by Kazakh herdsmen in Xinjiang Uygur AR.

Opposite top:
Gentians bring a slash of colour to a roadside alpine pasture near Jiuzhaigou in Sichuan.

Opposite centre:
Puffballs grow on grassland areas near Kanas Lake, where horses accidentally disperse their spores by kicking the fungi as they graze.

Opposite below:
A massed carpet of primulas and buttercups thrive on an ungrazed wet grassland at Napa Hai in Yunnan.

Over a quarter of the country's grasslands occur in the Inner Mongolia AR, which spans the centre of northern China. Variable rainfall over the region influences the grassland types and produces distinct vegetation zones. The tallest and most productive type is meadow grassland at the eastern edge of the Inner Mongolia AR, which extends into what was known as Manchuria (the three provinces of the north-east – Heilongjiang, Jilin and Liaoning). To the west of the Daxinganling Mountains are grasslands of medium height. Further west, short grasses grow in the dry grassland region; while to the south west of Wulanchabu and Ordos Plateaux is the desert grassland.

Inner Mongolia AR is well endowed with grasslands, but their quality has declined. In the nineteenth century, Han agriculturalists began moving into this region to cultivate the marginal land, reducing the grazing area. During the Great Leap Forward (1958-1960) and the following two decades, many Han migrants were transferred to the border areas to grow grain. The high precipitation (300-400 millimetres) and vegetation cover of the steppe could have sustained a gradual increase in both people and livestock; but such a rapid increase and loss of grazing area resulted in the vegetation becoming degraded.

Above:
Grassy patches on drier ungrazed slopes above the Napa Hai plain are natural wildflower gardens with wonderful mixtures of incarvilleas, asters and androsaces.

The story is much the same in the other grassland areas with different emphasis on the reasons behind the grassland destruction. Xinjiang Uygur AR is very dry, with less than 150 millimetres of precipitation per year. The herders move from mountain slopes in summer to dry basin rims in winter, where the yield is low, although it can be boosted if cut fodder is stored for winter use. In the past, the herders were true nomads, constantly moving with their herds so that the grasslands were not overgrazed.

In 2003, a national project was launched to protect the grasslands, whereby it was proposed that 66.7 million hectares of degraded grassland in the Inner Mongolia AR, north-west Xinjiang Uygur AR and Tibet AR should be removed from grazing within the next five years. The policy of dividing the Inner Mongolia AR grasslands into smaller plots, begun in the 1980s, forced herders to become settlers but some have

now merged their pastures to create a semi-nomadic way of life. Suggestions have been made about reverting back to a nomadic way of life, which allowed a more sustainable ecosystem, but this is hardly feasible when only 20 per cent of herders in Inner Mongolia AR are able horse riders – the rest now use motorcycles.

As China's deserts and grasslands become more accessible with new highways and airports being built, so the pressures will increase on these unique and vulnerable ecosystems. The immense challenge of balancing the long-term needs of wildlife, local people and increasing tourist numbers, will therefore require a multidisciplinary approach.

Above right:
This yurt on Tian Shan is the traditional house of nomadic herders, which move to higher or lower pastures with the seasons.

Right:
The bulbous nose of the saiga antelope is thought to filter out airborne dust during summer migrations and to heat the cold air before it reaches the lungs in winter.

DESERT PLANTS

Left:
Mouse melons – fruits of caper found in deserts in China – are sold for use in Chinese medicine.

Opposite:
1. Dodder (*Cuscuta* sp.) growing as a parasite on standing milkvetch (*Astragalus adsurgens*) near Turpan.

2. The bizarre fruit of a *Calligonum* growing in the desert near Turpan has stiff branching bristles, which aid wind dispersal.

3. Curious wax-like flowers of saxaul appear on new sappy stems, which are browsed by camels.

4. Golden sea lavender, common in sandy parts of China's northern deserts, is used to enhance the blood with invigorating and activating properties.

5. Star plum (*Calligonum* sp). flowering in the desert near Turpan, Xinjiang Uygur AR.

6. Flowering branches of tamarisk add splashes of pink to the desert landscape – especially along riverbanks.

7. A beetle feeds on petals of caper flower in the desert near Turpan, Xinjiang Uygur AR – the beginning of a desert food chain.

The range of plants found in deserts tends to be limited because they have to survive long periods of drought and extreme temperatures. Therefore, with the exception of plants that hug river courses, they tend to be succulents or drought-adapted perennials or shrubs. Some, such as *Calligonum*, appear to have dispensed with leaves altogether with their mass of green photosynthetic stems.

Succulent plants are able to live in arid climates by storing water in special storage organs in their leaves, stems or roots. Plants that are adapted in different ways to survive in places with little water are known as xerophytes. Cacti living in the New World deserts are good examples of xerophytic plants. Adaptations to dry surroundings can vary from one plant to another. Cutting down water loss is essential and this may be done with a hairy or waxy coating and by reducing the number of stomata (tiny pores for gaseous exchange) on the leaf surface, which cuts down water loss by evaporation.

One of China's most important xerophytic plants found in deserts is the saxaul, which is typically a large shrub, but may grow to be a sizable tree. The small, grey leaves are so insignificant the plant appears to be leafless. Within the Gobi desert the saxaul is typically the only tree in sight and the wood is useful in

several ways. Nomads have for long collected it for heating and cooking as it burns slowly like coal and, indeed, is known as 'coal of the desert'. The bark, which is soft and spongy, contains water that is extracted for drinking by pressing several layers of bark. Saxaul is an important plant aiding the stabilisation of sand dunes and has been extensively planted as shelter belts to stop the movement of sand dunes and to counteract desertification. It is also a popular food of camels.

In spring, flowering spikes of *Cistanche deserticola* begin to appear beside some saxaul, on which it lives as a root parasite in Gansu, Inner Mongolia AR, Qinghai and Xinjiang Uygur AR. Known as 'ginseng of the desert', the dried fleshy stem has been prized as an herbal medicine for 2,000 years. Collection of 450-550 tons of *Cistanche* per year and of the woody stems of its host – saxaul – is now threatening this curious desert parasite, which lacks chlorophyll.

Another woody plant is tamarisk (*Tamarix* spp.). Well adapted to arid climates with small leaves and extensive roots, it can survive on very poor soil, thereby helping to stabilise the sand, and also to make effective wind breaks. It can, however, out-compete smaller, less invasive species and the extensive root system can utilise a lot of water. In Xinjiang Uygur AR, it is known

as red willow from the reddish-brown bark of younger plants. The Botanic Garden at Turpan has a wide range of arid desert plants, including a special tamarisk collection where half of the Chinese species are grown.

As the caper (*Capparis spinosa*) grows in China's sandy deserts it begins to trap sand, eventually forming characteristic mounds with long shoots spreading out from the margins. This plant is widespread in other parts of Asia and also Europe, where the buds are collected for pickling for use as a gourmet condiment. The large cream flowers have outsized stamens.

Amongst the many species of *Calligonum* that occur in Chinese deserts – eight are endemic. They are the most conspicuous shrubs in active sand dunes where they help to stabilise the sand in north-east China. The tiny flowers produce four-angled nuts decorated either with wings or with a branching network of bristles, which buoys up the fruits so they are readily bowled by wind across the sand.

Related to the purple-flowered sea lavenders, which colonise salt marshes in Europe, golden sea lavender, *Limonium aureum*, is a dense dichotomously-branched perennial plant with bright yellow flowers that dominates stabilised sand fields in China's northern deserts.

5

Mountains

The scale of China's largest mountain ranges that remain snow-clad throughout the year are impressive in both their extent and height. Melt waters from snow and glaciers on these peaks feed many rivers. In addition to the classical single peaks, China has several intriguing multi-peaked mountains that contain a myriad of pillars, often eroded into bizarre shapes.

After a heavy overnight snowfall, the sun rises over the 4,140 metre-high summit of the pass on Jiajin Mountain in Sichuan.

Above:
A male Lady Amherst's pheasant is a striking but secretive bird.

Below right:
Rhododendron decorum growing in a forest at 3,000 metres in Yunnan.

Opposite:
Primula chionantha in an alpine meadow, Yunnan.

Most of China's highest mountain ranges run from north-west to south-east; they include Altai in the north-west and the Himalayas in the south-west. These ranges act as barriers, holding back air currents. Both the orientation of the ranges and the direction of the prevailing winds affect the climate and hence the vegetation cover. Because the mountains tend to run from west to east, they form latitudinal barriers separating distinct temperature zones. Moist air blowing down from the Arctic affects the northern slopes of the Tian Mountains (Tian Shan) in Xinjiang Uygur AR where spruce forests flourish, whereas the arid southern slopes are covered with dry steppe vegetation.

The Himalayas are even more effective at blocking the moist air carried by the south-west monsoon from reaching the Qinghai-Tibetan Plateau. This is evident in satellite images, which show the southern windward slopes with a high rainfall are covered with lush forests, in contrast to the dry prairie slopes of the northern slopes in the rain shadow.

The Hengduan Mountain system is one of China's few north-south ranges. Lying in the centre of the country, deeply incised river valleys separate a series of parallel ridges which rise up between the east of Tibet AR and the west of the Yunnan Plateau. This eco-region contains many rare animals including red pandas, clouded leopards (*Neofelis nebulosa*), Yunnan snub-nosed monkeys (*Rhinopithecus bieti*), musk deer and the secretive Lady Amherst's pheasant.

In the southern Hengduan Mountains are the Yulong Snow Mountain Nature Protection Area and Haba Nature Reserve. Yulong (Jade Dragon) Snow Mountain (5,596 metres) is the highest peak on the south bank of the Yangtze River and is thought to look like a flying dragon covered with snow. Haba's highest peak also exceeds 5,000 metres; with moraine lakes, cirques and glaciers present, there is snow and ice present year round.

However, Gaoligong Mountain NNR, which lies within the Three Parallel Rivers WHS on the west bank of the Nujiang River on the Sino-Myanmar border, is the jewel in the crown. This mountain range forms a divide between the rivers Nujiang (Salween) to the east and the Irawaddy to the west. It is also the watershed for these two great rivers and is famed for its waterfalls, some of which form multiple terraces. The Yangtze and upper Mekong rivers converge where the mountains meet the Nujiang River gorge.

ALPINE FLOWERS

There is no precise definition of an alpine flower apart from the fact that it has special adaptations that enable it to survive the harsh living conditions required to grow at high altitude. These include severe winds, poor soils, great fluctuations between day and night time temperatures, a short growing season and long, cold winters. Many alpines have extensive root systems or hairy stems or leaves, which help to preserve heat and cut down the water loss caused by severe winds. Others gain protection from the wind by being prostrate or by growing on the lee side of rocks or shrubs. As the atmosphere is thinner at altitudes of 4,000-5,000 metres, alpine plants also need to protect themselves against the harmful effects of ultra-violet (UV) light. For example, the snow lotus has leaves or bracts covered with hundreds of white hairs, which reflect these harmful rays from the sun. Other plants are protected from UV by a red pigment, anthocyanin, that absorbs the UV light before it can damage the leaves.

There is always a great sense of achievement in climbing several thousand metres in search of exquisite alpine flowers. All of the flowers illustrated on this spread have been photographed in Yunnan at elevations above 3,500 metres. True alpines have a comparatively short growing season. They need to grow, flower and produce seed in the few months between snowmelt and the first snow of autumn/winter.

China has many choice alpines, notably in Yunnan, Sichuan and on the Qinghai-Tibetan

Plateau. Among the perennials are the primulas, of which 300 of the known 500 species grow in China. They can be found along the banks of streams, in wet meadows, in marshy ground and even in damp crevices.

Finding a single specimen of any alpine for the first time is always exciting, but seeing a carpet of primulas flowering *en masse* is especially rewarding.

Gentians may be either annual or perennial and almost half of the known 500 species grow in China. Then there are the woody rhododendrons, of which China has over two thirds of the known 900 species. They range in size from diminutive alpine species no more than a few centimetres high, to huge trees such as those that form the impressive forest on Gaoligong Shan.

The Himalayan mayapple or eight-cornered lily (*Podophyllum hexandrum*) produces its flowers in spring before the leaves have fully grown. By the time the latter have expanded, the flowers have set fruit. The rhizomes contain podophyllin, a potentially deadly neurotoxin, which is incorporated into some commercial laxatives for its drastic purgative and emetic properties.

Choice flowers growing at high elevations include several species of *Meconopsis*, which belong to the poppy family, *Papaveraceae*. Their petal colour varies from the blue of the famed Himalayan blue poppy (*M. betonicifolia*) the red in *M. punicea*, the yellow *M. integrifolia* and *M. pseudointegrifolia*, to the pale lilac flowers of *M.*

racemosa. Tibetan doctors use many *Meconopsis* for medicinal purposes.

Some of the rarer and newly discovered alpine species are being cultivated in botanical gardens both in China and overseas to preserve their stock. Many others are available online or from garden centres to cultivate either from seed or seedlings, although in some cases growing them is a challenge because of the difficulties of replicating the precise montane conditions within a temperate garden.

Left:
A drift of *Primula sikkimensis* in a wet meadow in June.

Opposite:
1. Edelweiss *Leontopodium* sp. has a mass of tiny flowers on a central disc with conspicuous bracts.

2. *Rhododendron telmateium* is a dwarf alpine shrub with lavender flowers and grey-green leaves covered with golden scales.

3. The blousy pale yellow flowers of *Meconopsis pseudointegrifolia* are often to be found growing up through juniper bushes, where grazing stock leave them.

4. Like all euphorbias this one, which was growing on a natural cliff overlooking the grassland at Napa Hai NR, produces a white latex sap when the stem or leaves are damaged.

5. The compact fiery head of *Androsace bulleyana* is easily spotted on the sloping banks it favours. George Forrest collected this species and named it after the sponsor of his first expedition, Arthur K. Bully.

6. Himalayan mayapple with flowers and fruits; the new red leaves are still hanging vertically, tightly pressed to the stem.

7. *Meconopsis pratii* was growing in a natural rock garden overlooking the wet grassland within Napa Hai NR.

8 and 9. Slipper orchids (*Cypripedium flavum*), in Napa Hai NR, near Shangri-La or Zhongdian.

10. *Incarvillea compacta* produces deep pink trumpet-shaped flowers from a remarkably small plant. It belongs to the *Bignoniaceae* family which includes mostly trees and lianas.

Basalt columns, volcanic cones plus abundant hot springs within the Gaoligong Mountain area, are testimony of past and present geothermal activities. With three distinct climatic zones – subtropical, warm and frigid – Gaoligong is a biodiversity hotspot and is home to a plethora of plants and animals including the hoolock gibbon (*Hylobates leuconedys*), the slow loris (*Nycticebus coucang bengalensis*) as well as silver and golden pheasants, peacocks and sunbirds. This MAB reserve is recognised as the epicentre of plant endemism in north-west Yunnan, with camphor trees and camellias thriving in the evergreen forest that covers the east and west of the mountain. Rainfall increases with altitude from just over 700 millimetres on the east slope at 755 metres to almost 4,000 millimetres at 1,440 metres. Tree ferns abound and impressive *Rhododendron protistum* var. *giganteum* forests bloom in spring festooned with epiphytic mosses.

Rising up from the trailing southern end of the Hengduan Mountains is Chang Shan or Diancang Shan, reaching down on the east to Erhai Lake and on the west to the Heihuijiang River. Amongst the plant hunters who came here were Père Delavay, Frank Kingdom Ward, Joseph Rock and George Forrest; naturalists are still attracted to the rich botanical treasures including an array of rhododendrons, magnolias, *Pleione* orchids and arisaemas. Chang Shan is also famed for the Dali marble that is quarried here. This marble is renowned for its distinctive patterns and colours. The finest examples are made into screens that resemble a Chinese classical landscape.

Above:
Jade Dragon Snow Mountain at dawn, Yunnan.

Left:
A splendid green peacock perches in a tree.

Right:
Sectioned Dali marble resembles mountain scenery in Chinese landscape paintings.

KARST

The word karst originates from the karst plateau of eroded limestone rocks in Slovenia. Within a karst area, water dissolves limestone and carries calcium bicarbonate to re-deposit it as travertine (calcium carbonate) either underground in caves or on the surface. The South China Karst region, an extensive area

Yunnan, 80 kilometres south-east from the capital Kunming. This, the world's best example of a stone forest, covers an area of 350 square kilometres. Some 270 million years ago the area was a huge sea and when the limestone deposits were uplifted the rocks gradually became eroded and sculpted into magnificent and varied shapes.

notable features: the Qingkou Giant Doline (sinkhole), the Three Natural Bridges and the Furong Cave.

Another popular karst landscape is in the Guilin/Yangshuo region (yet to be proposed as a WHS). This appears as dramatic weathered karst peaks rising up from the flat cultivated plain.

chiefly within Yunnan, Guizhou and Guangxi Zhuang AR, (with a major extension into parts of Chongqing, Sichuan, Hunan, Hubei and Guangdong) became inscribed on UNESCO's World Heritage List as recently as June 2007. It is regarded as one of the most impressive humid tropical to subtropical karst landscapes in the world.

The diversity of this region is unrivalled and consists of three clusters: Shilin Karst, Libo Karst and the Wulong Karst. The most visited is the Stone Forest (Shilin) Geopark, which lies in

In places, the odd tree appears behind the upthrusting grey peaks and ridges – some with knife-sharp edges – while vines scramble up and over the rocks. Quite separate from the main stone forest is the Naigu (Black) Stone Forest where the rocks are darker but have also been eroded into dramatic shapes.

The Libo Karst region in Guizhou has a great variety of karst cones and towers clothed in forest, as well as deep sinkholes and extensive river caves. South-east from Chongqing is the Wulong Karst National Geopark, which has three

They are equally striking whether seen from the air or the ground and dominate the land from Guilin to Yangshuo with the picturesque Lijiang meandering between them. The rocks are made from Devonian limestone, which formed under the sea and became uplifted when the Himalayas were created. The isolated peaks in the Guilin area are known as *fenglin*, while towers linked at the base to form peak clusters are referred to as *fengcong*.

But there is much more to the Guilin area. Hidden beneath the surface are a galaxy of caves where the most impressive development of stalactites and stalagmites are lit with a kaleidoscope of coloured lights. Notable caves around the Guilin area include the Reed Flute Cave (*Ludi yan*) opened in 1962, the multi-storied Silver Cave opened in 1999 and the most recently discovered Green Lotus Cave.

Another extensive cave area lies to the west in Yunnan, north of the Stone Forest. Here, the 600 million-year-old Jiuxiang Cave is reached via a dramatic elevator, which descends to where the Maitian River thunders through a narrow gorge into the cave entrance. Eventually the system opens up into the huge 15,000 square metre Lion's Hall where a subterranean concert was held in 1999. Other notable features at Jiuxiang are a twin underground waterfall, the Fairy Palace filled with stalactites and stalagmites and the largest area of travertine terraces found within a cave, known as the Fairy Paddy Fields.

At Jiuzhaigou and Huanglong in Sichuan, most of the limestone has been eroded, transported by rivers downstream and re-deposited as travertine dams, waterfalls and terraces. Huanglong has over 3,300 brightly coloured pools, which cascade over travertine terraces and shoals plus a cave with many chambers and underground streams

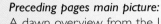

Preceding pages main picture:
A dawn overview from the Lion Pavilion of the Stone Forest Geopark in Yunnan, with spring foliage interspersed between the eroded grey limestone rocks.

Preceding page:
Limestone rock eroded into the shape of a bear in Wansheng Stone Forest in Chongqing.

Left:
The eroded limestone Stone Forest or Shilin is an extensive area of karst scenery, south-east of Kunming, which has been known since the Ming Dynasty.

Opposite:
1. Part of the extensive travertine terrace at Huanglong in Sichuan.

2. The Music Screen is one of the impressive formations in the multi-storied Silver Cave near Yangshuo.

3. Stalactites and stalagmites inside the Fairy Palace, Jiuxiang Cave in Yunnan, lit by coloured lights.

4. Travertine terraces, known as Fairy Paddy Fields, inside Jiuxiang Cave in Yunnan.

Below:
The blind subterranean fish, *Sinocyclocheilus*, lives in Jiuxiang Cave. It has a distinct bump on the head and barbels for feeling along the bottom, but no eyes.

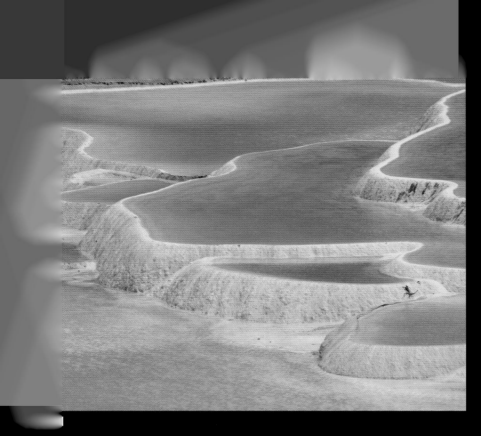

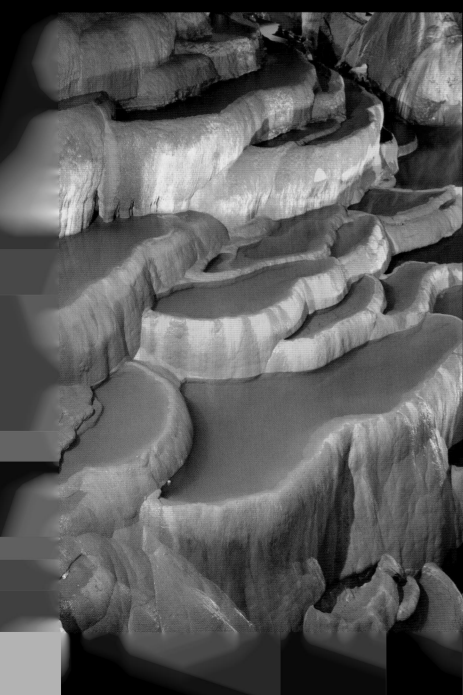

2

Chang Tang Wildlife Reserve in the north-west of Tibet AR on the central Tibetan Plateau, is one of the largest nature reserves in the world and was established in 1993. Most of it lies at an altitude of 4,400-5,000 metres and includes some mountains over 6,000 metres. Because of the intense cold, the vegetation is sparse, so the alpine steppes are unable to support agriculture or forests; therefore some of the most pristine ecosystems in temperate Eurasia exist here. Herds of wild ungulates roam the reserve with their predators not far behind. Blue sheep, argalis and wild yak favour grazing the mountain slopes; whereas kiang or Tibetan wild asses, chiru or Tibetan antelopes – which are endemic to the Tibetan Plateau – and Tibetan gazelles prefer to live on the open plains. The blue sheep, which have a grey coat with a bluish tinge, are able to move with great agility over rocky slopes. In May, pregnant female Tibetan antelopes together with female calves born the previous year, form huge herds and migrate north to birthing grounds outside the reserve, where their synchronous birthing minimises loss of calves to predators.

It is difficult to distinguish between true wild yak, feral animals and the hybrid dzos. At one time, it was thought that most of the true wild yaks had become extinct, but large herds have since been found in remote areas. Most of the predators, which include lynx, snow leopards and brown bears are protected from hunting, but no such protection is extended to wolves. There are also many smaller mammals, which are preyed upon by both mammalian and avian predators. These include Tibetan woolly hares (*Lepus oiostrolus*), Himalayan marmots, (*Marmota himalayana*) and black-lipped pika (*Ochotoma curzoniae*). The pika is a colonial animal that lives in burrows. Recent research has found that the root vole (*Microtos oeconomus*), which is widespread in the Chang Tang, manages to survive winters without hibernation by having a low body temperature combined with a high metabolic rate.

Holy mountains

In ancient China, many mountains were considered to be holy. They even lured emperors to make sacrifices, inspired scholars to write poetry and attracted people to worship. Well laid out trails with endless steps lead up to temples with tea pavilions en route. In the east lie China's five sacred Taoist mountains. They were declared to be sacred by the Han Emperor Wu Di in the second century BC. They are referred to collectively as *Wuyue*. Taoism was the original indigenous religion of China and the layout of these Taoist mountains relates to the five cardinal directions of Chinese geomancy (*feng shui*), which believes a sacred force, known as the dragon current, runs through the Earth and can be either *yin* (female) or *yang* (male). Mountains are believed to be powerful sites of primarily the *yang* component. The mountain in the east is Tai Shan (Shandong); in the west is Hua Shan (Shaanxi); in the south is Heng Shan (Hunan); in the north is Heng Shan, also in Shaanxi and in the centre Song Shan (Henan). Tai Shan being the easternmost, receives light from the rising sun first and so is regarded as the most sacred of the five; so sacred that 72 emperors are recorded as having visited it.

Opposite:
A captive-bred snow leopard leaps from a snow-covered ridge; the outsized paws function as snow shoes.

Opposite below:
A yak hybrid mother checks out her newborn calf.

Below:
Yak grazing in front of snow-capped Gungar Shan on the Qinghai-Tibetan Plateau.

Buddhism was introduced to China in the first century BC. There are four major Buddhist sacred mountains; in descending height they are: Emei Shan (Sichuan); Wutai Shan (Shaanxi); Jiuhua Shan (Anhui) and the smallest is the mountain island of Putuo Shan, off the Zhejiang coast.

Emei Shan is the highest of all the nine sacred mountains and is also famous as one of the richest botanical mountains in the northern hemisphere. It is the best place to see fragments of the Sichuan Basin subtropical forests and their wildlife. The plantsman, Roy Lancaster, has a high regard for Emei Shan; 'If there is one mountain in China calculated to set a plantsman's pulse racing, it is Emei Shan.' The wingthorn rose (*Rosa omeiensis pteracantha*) originates from this mountain. It is not so much the small, white flowers that are the main attraction as the new shoots which have

Epiphytic mosses thrive on oaks and conifers in humid mixed forest, Little Snow Mountain Pass.

outsized red thorns that glow when backlit. The Emei Shan liocicla (*Liocichla omeiensis*) is a small bird restricted to Emei Shan and neighbouring hills. Tibetan stump-tailed macaques (*Macaca thibetana*) also occur here.

For centuries, all the holy mountains were protected by monasteries and were respected by the pilgrims who visited the temples. They were tranquil places of retreat where sustainable forestry was practised, so they became safe refuges for wildlife; in

Above top right:
Paeonia lutea growing on wet scree in Yunnan.

Above right:
Wingthorn rose produces huge red wing-shaped thorns each spring.

contrast to their surrounding natural lowlands which were lost to agriculture. These holy mountains survived the Cultural Revolution, but now they are threatened by pressure from tourists because sacred mountains are big business. Climbing the many steps with shallow risers along the ancient pilgrim trails can be quite hazardous – especially in wet weather – as you compete with hordes of jostling visitors making their way up and down a mountain, along paths which have a sheer drop plunging down one side.

Some of the mountains – including Emei Shan – now have cable cars that whisk visitors virtually to the top. The cable cars with the passengers they carry not only disturb the wildlife but also take away the sense of achievement by struggling on foot to reach the summit. In certain weather conditions, it is possible to see the Buddha's halo from the top. This 'Spectre of Broken' forms when a low angled sun is shining behind a person on the mountain looking out into mist. The shadow of the figure in the mist forms the spectre as a shadow at the bottom of the halo, which forms directly opposite to the sun.

123

Opposite:
Huangshan pine trees on Huang Shan silhouetted at dawn.

Right:
Frog with eggs attached resting on wall on Emei Shan.

Far right:
A black-veined white butterfly (*Aporia hippia*) at Haba in Yunnan.

Below:
Longhorn beetle on rose, north Yunnan.

Scenic mountains

Huang Shan (Yellow Mountain) in Anhui is a WHS with an astonishing 72 named craggy granite peaks. The scenery is stunning and inspired a school of painting in the late Ming period. The surrounding landscape was once covered by the Yangtze Sea, which receded when the area was uplifted. Glaciers later eroded and sculpted the rocks, on many of which distorted pines, anchored in crevices cling to precipices. These two scenic elements – one inanimate and the other living – together form the classic Chinese landscape with slender peaks peppered with trees clinging precariously to them. For two thirds of the year, mist and clouds swirl around the peaks, offering tantalising glimpses of the scenery. On clear days, after rain or snow has fallen, the humid air creates a sea of clouds from which the taller peaks emerge dramatically. This drama is enhanced at first and last light when the rising or setting sun paints the scene with golden rays. Huang Shan has for long provided inspiration for literary scholars, poets and artists and is now a Mecca for photographers.

Two kinds of pine tree grow on Huang Shan; below 800 metres is the Masson pine (*Pinus massoniana*) and above 800 up to 1,800 metres is the Huangshan pine (*P. hwangshanensis*) which covers 56 per cent of the land. The most ancient 1,000-year-old trees are celebrated with individual names, as are other trees misshapen by constant wind pruning to produce gnarled branches and roots. Notable animal inhabitants include rhesus and stump-tailed macaques, Asiatic black bears, wild dogs, Chinese ferret-badgers (*Melogale moschata*), wild boar and pangolins (*Manis pentadactyla*).

Snow falls are not infrequent in winter. But the scenic drama of this unique topography is at its height during the few days when specific weather conditions result in spectacular frosty encrustations covering the underside of the pine trees. This occurs when moist air swirls around and freezes overnight building up into breathtaking ice sculptures on the pine needles. After summer rains, rainbows may appear above the sea of clouds. During summer thunderstorms, visitors are advised not to raise their umbrellas for fear of gusts of wind snatching them unawares and causing them to fall.

Wulingyuan Scenic Zone is a WHS in north-west Hunan. It consists of Zhangjiajie NP, the Suoxi Valley Reserve and the Tianzi Shan (Emperor Mountain) Reserve. The latter contains 3,000 sandstone pillars and peaks, (more eroded than the

granite peaks of Huang Shan) that tower above the canyons with waterfalls cascading into them. The scenery constantly changes as clouds swirl around the craggy peaks, or when snow falls or thick hoar frosts form in winter. Amongst the rare plants found in this area are the maidenhair tree and dawn redwood; and the rare animals include the clouded leopard, giant salamander and pangolin.

Siguniang Shan (Four Girls) Scenic Area is the highest part of the Qionglai Mountain range at the eastern end of the Hengduan Mountains in west Sichuan. It is a beautiful place in any season, but especially so when the snow-capped peaks rise up against a clear blue sky. Not surprisingly, it is known as the Alps of the Orient. Visitors can explore three valleys; one by coach which stops repeatedly and the others on foot or by horseback. In summer, the alpine meadows are carpeted with flowers and the many lakes in Alpine Lake (Haizi) Valley sparkle in the sunlight. Heavy snow can fall as early as September, which transforms the sombre ancient sea buckthorn (*Hippophae rhamnoides*) trees with their broad crowns in Two-Bridge (Shuangqiao) Valley. The orange fruits of the sea buckthorn persist through winter, providing a valuable food source for many birds.

Above:
Huang Shan landscape at dusk.

Right:
The Eurasian lynx preys on hares and pikas in
montane regions throughout much of China.

Far right:
Rhesus macaque monkey at forest edge, Wolong.

Opposite:
Veteran sea buckthorn tree after heavy snowfall
on Siguniang Shan.

Above top:
Assam indigo leaves are grown in Guizhou to produce the dark blue dye used by several minority groups.

Above:
Tubs with Assam indigo leaves oxidised to form dark blue dye, Guizhou.

Left:
Mountain Miao minority girls from Fanpai village wear indigo dyed skirts and silver head-dresses at festivals.

Below:
Forming pleats in wax-resistant skirt dyed with Assam indigo worn by Bouyei minority women, Guizhou.

Mountain Miao

With a population of almost nine million, the Miao are one of the largest ethnic minorities in south-west China, living mostly in hilly or mountainous areas. Dispersal and migration over the centuries has resulted in local variations within their dialect and traditional clothing; but the basic dress is plain indigo-dyed clothing decorated with embroidered collars, sleeve panels and trouser legs. During festivals and weddings, silver jewellery – including elaborate head-dresses – is worn. In Guizhou, silver is so esteemed by the Miao people they begin collecting for their daughter's dowry at her birth. Silver jewellery was first made in the Ming Dynasty from silver coins bought from traders. During the Cultural Revolution, the wearing of jewellery was forbidden; so all the silver was secreted away by burying it. Pure silver has now been replaced by a silver alloy or silver plate.

Above top:
Dry snow lotus (*Saussurea involucrata*) for sale as a medicinal herb in Xinjiang Uygur AR.

Above:
Ripe sea buckthorn fruits at Jiuzhaigou.

Below:
Dried caterpillar fungi attached to caterpillars of over-wintering moths which they parasitise.

In mountain regions, Miao houses are usually built of wood on slopes raised up on stilts, so the animals can be housed on the ground floor. Gradually the traditional straw or fir bark roofs are being replaced by tiles as the Miao become more prosperous. High up in mountainous areas, rice is grown using wooden pipes to carry stream water to irrigate the fields. Water-wheels are also used to raise water to even higher terraces. After the rice harvest, the Miao used to grow opium poppies (*Papaver somniferum*) as a cash crop to buy silver ornaments. Rape (*Brassica* spp.) and tobacco (*Nicotiana* spp.) gradually replaced opium, which was finally abolished in the 1950s. Now tourists, attracted to the Miao festivals, provide a cash income by buying their textiles and embroidery.

Medical mountain plants

Snow lotus (*Saussurea involucrata*) grows at elevations of 3,500-3,600 metres on Tian Shan looking more like a leafy cabbage than a type of daisy. A high alpine meadow with many snow lotus in bloom set against snow-covered peaks is a glorious sight. Fine hairs on the stem and bracts, plus a root that penetrates down to a depth of a metre, enable the snow lotus to flower and set seed even when snow blankets the ground. The flowers, complete with their leafy rosettes, are collected for sale as a traditional Chinese medicine. Dried plants are sold year-round for the treatment of rheumatoid arthritis, stomachache and altitude sickness. A Tibetan species, *Saussurea gossypiphora*, which looks like a snowball when young, has well-developed bracts densely covered with white woolly hairs that are tightly packed around the recessed flower buds to retain heat and help to protect the flowers from the severe winds.

Sea buckthorn fruits are high in vitamins C and E and have been used medicinally in China for at least twelve centuries; indeed they were much prized by Chinese emperors for revitalising their energy. An important natural resource of China's mountainous regions, this plant grows naturally in sandy soil at altitudes of 1,200-4,500 metres, but recently it has a new use; it has been extensively planted across much of northern China to stabilise sandy soils and halt desertification. Sea buckthorn forests planted in Liaoning increased the vegetation cover from four per cent in the 1950s to 34 per cent in the 1990s. This reduced run-off by 90 per cent and soil erosion by 70 per cent. In addition, the fruits are now being harvested from over one million hectares of wild sea buckthorn and almost 300,000 hectares of cultivated plants for commercial production as a juice and as a nutrient supplement. Legend has it that Genghis Khan fed these nutrition-packed berries to his soldiers and horses for strength before battle and to keep them healthy afterwards.

Another important mountain resource is the caterpillar fungus, which is a common parasite on the swift moth caterpillar in subalpine to alpine zones from 3,000 to 4,700 metres altitude. When the finger-like dark brown-black fruiting body of the fungus emerges above ground, collectors carefully dig each one out by hand so that it remains attached to the caterpillar host. Being regarded as an aphrodisiac, it is known as 'Himalayan Viagra' and it fetches a high price.

Sky burial

Sky burial is one of three prime ways that Tibetans traditionally return their dead to the earth. The two others are cremation and water burial. All three methods are still used today; the choice varies with the type of terrain, so that in towns with access to a river, water burial is performed by cutting a corpse into small pieces so they can be eaten by fish.

A sky burial (or *jhator* as it is known in Tibetan), is a practical solution to the problem of disposal of the dead in a land where the ground is often too hard to dig a grave. Drigung Monastery is one of the three most important *jhator* sites. When the Chinese government outlawed sky burials in the 1960s, they almost became a lost

tradition, but they were legalised once again in the 1980s. Children under eighteen, pregnant women, anyone who has died from an infectious disease, as well as robbers and murderers are not permitted a sky burial. High lamas are given a stupa burial after the body is painted with salt water and dried before being embalmed after it is smeared with ointments and perfumes.

After death, a body is prepared for a sky burial by placing it in a foetal position and wrapping it in a white cloth for three days before it is taken to the charnel grounds – usually near a monastery. Sky burial is a ritual whereby the corpse is offered to vultures known by Tibetans as Dakinis or 'sky dancers' who take the soul up to heaven. Himalayan griffon vultures are a bird of high mountain ranges which feed only on carrion. In Tibet AR, the vultures which feed on human corpses are regarded as holy birds and are strictly protected. These birds are so heavy they have to rely on updrafts to give them lift.

On the day of the sky burial, juniper is burnt to purify the air. The body is prepared for the vultures by the body breakers using sharp cleavers to dissect the flesh. As they step back, the vultures move in and soon devour the flesh. The vultures are then driven away so the skeleton can be broken with large mallets into small splinters, mixed with roasted barley flour or *tsampa* and thrown to waiting hawks and crows. The ascent of the soul is then complete.

Threats to mountains

Tibetan antelopes were once slaughtered in large numbers for their warm, soft wool – known as *shahtoosh*. This wool is so fine an entire shawl can be passed through a finger ring, but the wool can only be obtained by killing the animals, so the population has dropped from a million at the turn of the twentieth century to just 75,000 in the mid 1990s. Their commercial hunting was banned in Tibet AR from 1994 and this has enabled these antelopes (as well as the kiang) gradually to build up the size of their herds again, but illegal hunting still occurs. The once remote Tibetan Plateau is becoming more accessible – via improved roads and the opening of the high-speed railway in July 2006 connecting Beijing to Lhasa. The line climbs up to 5,072 metres at its highest point, making it the world's highest railway and bisects the chiru's feeding grounds, so in an effort to protect the Tibetan antelopes, thirty-three migration passages were constructed beneath the railway.

Above:
An aggressive male golden snub-nosed monkey bares its teeth.

However, environmentalists fear this new route into Tibet AR will threaten the high altitude fragile ecosystems, by giving illegal hunters using modern automated weapons greater access to the chiru's habitat and breeding grounds.

Likewise, many of China's summits are becoming much more accessible, even for short day trips by cable car. As the numbers of tourists spirals ever upwards, this puts increasing pressure on these special habitats. For alpine meadows with no easy access – apart from climbing up there on foot – tourists rarely visit and there is a different threat. As stock levels increase, these suffer increased grazing and trampling, which degrades the turf and associated alpines that have a short growing season.

But now in addition to the direct and indirect people pressures, mountains also face a threat from climate change, which is causing glaciers – notably in Yunnan – to recede. According to research done by the Nature Conservancy's Global Climate Change Institute, the Mingyong glacier on Mount Kawegebo, one of Tibet's

Above:
Epiphytic beard lichens are the main winter food of golden snub-nosed monkeys.

Below right:
The wolverine or glutton, the biggest member of the weasel family, has strong teeth for crushing frozen carrion.

Buddhist sacred mountains, has receded 530 metres in the last decade and since the late nineteenth century it has receded some 2.7 kilometres. Being a sacred glacier, core samples of the ice cannot be taken, but repeat photography is a useful non-invasive tool for recording the sites at which the glaciers are retreating and for measuring the annual rate of shrinkage.

Redressing the balance

Despite their grandeur and remoteness China's larger mountain ranges are vulnerable to the deprivations from human pressure. Here, the main threats are felling trees for fuel wood, unsustainable collection of animals and medicinal plants, over-grazing of stock on alpine pastures and insensitive tourist developments. Gradually, with help and guidance from conservation bodies, ways are being found to counteract these threats. The preservation of mountain forests plays a major role in preventing erosion and reducing serious flooding on the plains.

The introduction of solar power or biogas production to families in mountain villages, such as in Baima Snow Mountain Nature Reserve, has helped to reduce the trees felled for fuel for heating and cooking and are also boosting the income of local residents.

Over-collection of snow lotus plants in Xinjiang Uygur AR was threatening this special alpine plant with a staggering five million being sold annually. Now the region has set a limit of 500,000 packages, each one to contain two flowers. Also, the cultivation of snow lotus plants has begun in glasshouses for transplantation out into the open.

Taoist communities are now so concerned about the threats to all holy mountains that together with the Government Bureau of Religious Affairs and the Alliance of Religions and Conservation (ARC), they launched the Sacred Mountain Project. This project involved a major ecological survey of the main Taoist and Budddhist mountains. ARC has recommended that the Buddhist mountain, Wutai Shan, should be used as the model of how sacred mountains in China can be managed. On the other hand, the natural environment of Emei Shan is being destroyed by over-development. China is developing a chain of Buddha theme parks and Emei Shan is at risk of becoming engulfed by an upmarket version of this development. What is urgently needed is a balanced way of using these beautiful and unique mountains, so that they are not irreparably damaged.

6

Coastlines

For the most part, China's borders lie inland, so that this vast country has a comparatively small – yet varied – mainland coastline of some 18,000 kilometres, which is almost doubled when the offshore islands are included. The types of shore range from temperate rocky shores and sandy beaches in the north, via temperate and subtropical saline meadows as well as subtropical rocky shores to tropical mangroves, coconut-fringed beaches and coral reefs in the far south.

A spectacular rocky coastline runs around the far eastern tip of Shandong at Chenshantou.

Left:
Abalones (*Haliotus* sp.), which are popular seafood along the northern coast, have an inner nacre or iridescent mother of pearl layer.

Below:
A 200-year-old house in Rongcheng County, Shandong, with a 'seaweed' roof made from sea-grass, keeps the house warm in winter and cool in summer.

Opposite above:
A pair of whooper swans (*Cygnus cygnus*) display to each other by flapping their wings and calling whilst raising and lowering their bills, Rongcheng Swan NR.

Opposite below:
Whooper swans, which overwinter in sheltered bays at Rongcheng Swan NR in Shandong, gather to drink at a freshwater outlet.

China's mainland coastline stretches from 40° north on the Korean Peninsula down to 20° north on the eastern Vietnam border and is washed by four seas – the Bohai Sea, the Yellow Sea, the East China Sea and the South China Sea. From Hong Kong right up to Shanghai and beyond is extensively developed. Nonetheless, there are still some fine examples of coastal habitats and spectacular scenery.

The coast of China is hit by more typhoons than any other country – seven a year on average – which can strike from May to December, although they tend to be concentrated between July and September. They hit the coast south of the Yangtze River with Guangdong being the most prone region, but Fujian as well as Taiwan are also in the typhoon belt. When very heavy rain falls during a short period and large tidal waves make landfall, great damage and loss of life can result. Global warming is causing an increase in both the frequency of typhoons as well as their strength.

Geological feature

Where land meets sea and persistent wave action pounds hard cliffs, they gradually become eroded to form some dramatic scenery. South of Beihai city, in Guangxi Zhuang AR, on the southern coast, lies Weizhou Island, the largest and youngest volcanic island in China. The island was created from volcanic rock and lava during the Quaternary Period. The most dramatic coastal features occur in the southern and highest part of the island. Here pillars, terraces and arches intermingle with lava-eroded caverns. These provide sheltered havens for a multitude of marine life, some of which is visible when the sea recedes at low tide.

At the most eastern tip of Shandong Peninsula lies Chengshantou Scenery Park. Along the indented coastline steep cliffs, sea caves, gullies and rocky platforms have arisen as a result of pounding wave action accentuated by fierce storms. Surrounded by the sea on three sides, sailors give Chengshantou a wide berth. As the eastern-most

point of China's coastline, it is where the sunrise can be seen first in China, and is known as China's Cape of Good Hope. Just 94 sea miles away from South Korea, it was off the coast here that the Yellow Sea Battle took place in 1894-95 during the Sino-Japanese War.

Ten kilometres from Chengshantou is Rongcheng Swan NR, which includes bays where several thousand whooper swans and other birds come to overwinter. Most of the swans congregate in Yue Hu, now known as Swan Lake, flying back and forth from their feeding grounds. Their favourite food is *Zosterophyllum*, which is a marine flowering plant rather than a seaweed. The long green ribbon-like leaves were collected by local people to make the so called 'seaweed roofs' on their houses. Some of these are a hundred or more years old and are a feature of the Rongcheng area.

Across the sea, north-west from Chengshantou, is the Liaoning Peninsula with the busy port of Dalian at the southern tip. Originally a small fishing village, today it is an important trading and financial centre of north-east Asia and is often referred to as the 'Hong Kong of northern China'. Lying east of Beijing, Dalian boasts some stunning examples of coastal scenery. Along the 30-kilometre Jinshi Beach coastline which extends north-eastwards from Dalian, sandy beaches are interspersed by rocky headlands. Here, wind and waves have combined to sculpt natural arches and anthropomorphic-shaped rocks – many of which radiate a golden glow in sunlight or appear as striking silhouettes at dusk and dawn. This natural maritime stone forest dates back 600 million years to the Silurian Period when this area was a shallow sea. Within the rocks fossilised plants and animals – including ammonites – are to be found.

Slightly inland from Jinshi Beach, an area of submerged golden rocks was discovered in 1996 when excavations were begun for a hotel. It took a further five years digging to unearth the weathered rocks that now form the sunken Golden Rock NG. Paths – some very narrow – wind their way around intriguing shapes naturally sculpted aeons ago.

Rocky shores

Relatively sheltered rocky shores that are not constantly pounded by the surf are home to an array of molluscs, sea anemones, crustaceans and fish as well as seaweeds. These organisms do not occur haphazardly on the shore, but tend to live in distinct zones, depending on their tolerance of exposure to the air at low tide. Animals with hard outer shells that protect the inner soft tissues such as barnacles, limpets and various marine snails are typically found on bare rock. Soft-bodied sea anemones and sponges, on the other hand, occur in humid microhabitats beneath boulders, rocky overhangs or inside caves where there is no risk of drying out during exposure at low tide. As the tide recedes, crabs can retreat into rocky crevices or they may remain underwater in rock pools together with prawns and fish.

The size and shape of pools on these shores is determined by the topography of the rocks and their strata. The simplest pools, with least variety of life, are shallow depressions high up on the shore where they can be subjected to wide fluctuations in temperature and salinity. On a hot day the seawater soon warm ups, while a heavy deluge during low tide dilutes the salinity of the seawater. Large deeper pools where seaweeds flourish support a much wider variety of marine organisms, which can shelter beneath the seaweed fronds.

Off Zhejiang and just 150 kilometres from Taiwan, Nanji Islands is a marine archipelago comprising 23 islands and 69 reefs. This was one of five marine reserves to be declared in China in 1990. Just eight years later it became the first marine MAB Reserve in this country. Nanji Islands are especially interesting because they lie at the interface between temperate and tropical zones and at the junction where the Jiangsu-Zhejiang coastal current and the warm Kuroshio or Taiwan Current alternatively fluctuate. Plankton sampling in Nanji waters has shown there is a seasonal change in the zooplankton species as a result of this fluctuation. The Kuroshio Current flows along the east coast of Taiwan north-eastwards past Japan, where it merges with the easterly drift of the North Pacific Current.

Above:
Encrusting sponges live beneath boulders, in rock crevices or on the underside of overhangs.

Right:
A natural window formed in warm-coloured rocks within the Golden Rock NG at Dalian.

Below:
Small gastropod snails left exposed by the receding tide, cluster together in empty oyster shells.

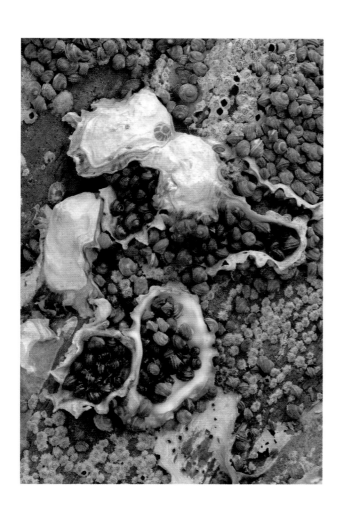

It is analogous to the North Atlantic Drift or Gulf Stream in the Atlantic Ocean, transporting warm, tropical water northward towards the polar region.

Nanji Islands have an oceanic monsoon climate with an average annual temperature of 16.5°C. A diverse range of marine habitats support an astonishing 403 species of shellfish – fifteen of which are confined to Nanji – and 174 different kinds of marine algae, some of which are edible and have medicinal properties. Because the islands straddle two climatic zones, they present an important location for marine biologists to monitor the northern migration of southern marine life and the southern migration of northern marine life – especially in relation to climate change. Nanji Island is the largest one in the group; at the southern cape of Dasha'ao the main beach reserve area is formed of fine shell sand. Offshore lies Longchuan Reef where a rare black Sargassum seaweed grows. In July and August the seawater around Nanji Islands is clear and an attractive blue colour, whereas come autumn and winter it's much more turbid with a distinct yellow tinge.

Sandy beaches

Sandy beaches occur in large bays and small coves where tidal currents allow the deposition and build up of sand particles broken down from rock or shell gravel from the fragmentation of marine shells. The colour of these beaches varies from white to yellow and gold and even black. Pure sand beaches – whatever their colour – which are so popular with tourists support little marine life since the worms and shellfish which burrow into soft beaches need to feed on detritus.

One of the most beautiful beaches in China is the 3,500-metre-long crescent shaped Jinshatan (Golden Sand Beach) on the south-east of Xuejia Isle off Qingdao in Shandong. Twice as long is the white sand beach at Yalong Bay to the east of Sanya city in the south of Hainan Island. This tropical island has an average air temperature of 26°C and the seawater temperature never drops below 22°C. Where the South China Sea water covers the white sand both here and at nearby Dadonghai Bay, it appears a stunning aquamarine colour.

Changli Golden Beach in north-east Hebei is a spectacular golden sandy beach. Instead of a flat expanse, sand dunes – some reaching up to 44 metres high – overlook the beach. The dunes which extend over an area of 300 square kilometres and date back 2,000-3,000 years are still increasing in size as sand carried by the Liugu River is discharged into the Bohai Sea where currents carry it south-west before it ends up on the west coast of the Bohai Gulf. Winds then carry the sand inland adding to the height of the dunes.

Several sandy beaches occur in Hong Kong, Repulse Bay being the best known and most popular. White sand beaches in Hong Kong include Tai Long Wan on the east of Sai Kung Peninsula, Kwun Yam Beach on the east coast of Cheung Chau and Fan Lau on Lantau Island. Hac Sa (Black Sand) Beach on Macau no longer lives up to its name, since the Government added golden sand, when the original black sand was in danger of disappearing due to erosion.

Above:
The incoming sea gently laps the extensive Jinsha (Golden Sand) beach at Dalian.

Below:
Tentacles of a sea anemone grasp a crab in a rock pool low down on the shore at Dalian.

Above:
Bivalves such as these edible 'flying clams' live buried in muddy-sand with their siphons protruding.

Below:
Sub-zero winter temperatures result in ice forming along the shoreline of the Yellow Sea saline meadows and in creeks as here in Yancheng NNR.

Saline meadows

Where silt-laden rivers shed their load onto sheltered coastlines, a completely different kind of coastal habitat – known as saline meadows – develops. The Yellow Sea saline meadow has built up from deposits made by the Yangtze and Huai He rivers. In between these river mouths lies the transition zone between temperate and subtropical climates.

The silt deposits are home to a wide range of marine invertebrates – including worms, bivalves and crustaceans that burrow into the fine mud. Once the tide recedes to reveal small creeks, mudskippers (*Periophthalmus*) can be seen skimming over the water surface to reach a nearby bank where they can crawl using their limb-like pectoral fins. The exposed mud flats attract a vast number of resident waders as well as winter visitors and migrant birds. Many use it as a stopover to refuel en route along the East Asian-Australasian flyway. Offshore, one of the worlds four largest breeding colonies of Saunders's gull (*Larus saundersi*) occurs.

The dominant plant on the mudflats is a succulent, known as goosefoot (*Suaeda salsa*), which adds vibrant colour to otherwise rather drab surroundings. This plant is one of the most important halophytes (salt-loving plants) in China. The flats are inundated by salt water at each high tide, which rises quickly over these flat saline meadows. This coast has a high annual rainfall of 800-1,200 millimetres and is prone to typhoons. The importance of this region has been recognised by the declaration of Yancheng in Jiangsu as a MAB reserve. Half of the world's population of elegant red-crowned cranes (see pages 78, 86) overwinter here, together with other cranes, the rare black-faced spoonbill (*Platalea minor*) and the Baikal teal (*Anas formosa*).

FOOD FROM THE SEA

Maritime communities the world over have a ready supply of fresh protein. The night fish market in Dalian where fisherman sell their catches to traders, provides an insight into the varied marine life which is eaten by local inhabitants and served up at restaurants. As overfilled boxes are unloaded from baskets on bicycles and containers on trucks, the floor becomes awash with a layer of slippery ice. On the Jiaodong Peninsula in Shandong across the water from Dalian seafoods are also a popular local speciality.

On a much smaller scale, beachside traders offer a wide assortment of marine life for sale in plastic bowls kept alive with battery-operated aerators. In one location alone adjacent to the famous Jinshi Beach near Dalian, the choice may include crabs, prawns, starfish, sea urchins, scallops, cockles, razor shells, sea cucumbers, abalones, octopuses, mantis shrimp, oysters and

a variety of marine snails, not to mention an assortment of fish. Seaweeds are also widely eaten in China, both thin sheets of the green alga known as sea lettuce as well as large brown kelps with a high iodine content, which helps to prevent goitre.

After large-scale collection of natural resources in many coastal locations, mariculture has developed from the production of just four species of molluscs to include other shellfish, crustaceans, algae (seaweeds) and also fish. To boost the stock of large yellow croaker (*Pseudosciaena crocea*) – a fish considered a great delicacy – over six million fry have been released annually over a five-year period off the Zhejiang coast.

The brown kelp *Laminaria japonica* is the most economic seaweed in China, which started to be cultured in 1952. It is cultivated on floating rafts that are firmly anchored to wooden stakes driven into the seabed. After shellfish cultivation became a reality in the late 1980s, many fishermen turned to shellfish farming and the volume of seaweed production dropped. Kelp is a health food and also a source of alginates and iodine. Nitrogen and phosphorus are needed for kelp growth and suitable conditions are found off Fujian, Zhejiang and Jiangsu provinces.

Economically important shellfish include oysters (*Crassostrea plicatula*) and the abalone (*Haliotis discus*) that contains several vitamins, which help to improve the body's immune system.

1

2

7

3

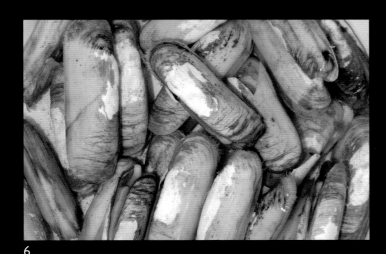

6

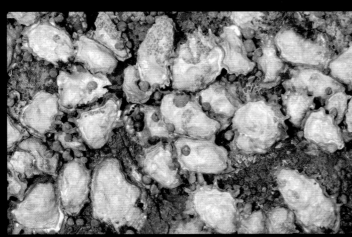

5

4

For millions of years this highly productive region was known as the land of fish
and rice, but Jiangsu is the most crowded area in China (with a population density
of 725 people per square kilometre in 2000). Now, the coastline is threatened by the
development of shrimp-rearing ponds, salt production and commercial reedbeds.
A future threat is the reclamation of land for industrial as well as recreational
development. The construction of the Three Gorges Dam has reduced the amount
of water and silt loads reaching the delta.

Further north, lies the temperate Bohai Sea saline meadow within the mouths
of the Luan He and the Huang He rivers to the west of the Shandong Peninsula.
Migrating birds also use this area to refuel. The deposition of sediment from the
Yellow River (see page 66) constantly encroaches into the Bohai Sea, increasing the
area of this saline meadow at a rate of 50 square kilometres per year.

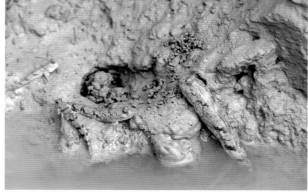

Mangroves

Mangroves flourish on tropical and subtropical coasts on enclosed intertidal mudflats close to freshwater outflows, where wave action is much reduced and the average temperature does not drop below 19°C. A complex branching network of substantial mangrove roots helps to stabilise the mud. The value of mangroves as an important buffer zone between the land and the tidal sea became all too evident after the Asian Boxing Day tsunami in 2004, when areas with an intact mangrove belt suffered much less damage compared with shorelines where the mangroves had been uprooted.

Dongzhaigang NNR on the north of Hainan Island has the richest assortment of mangrove species in China. The marine life that inhabits the mud banks include fiddler crabs (*Uca*), which emerge from their burrows at low tide, shrimps, shellfish, sipunculid or peanut worms and oysters. Juvenile fish are protected within this sheltered habitat that attracts 159 species of birds, some of which use the mangrove branches close to the water as convenient perching posts to search for fish. Dongzhaigang has a mangrove restoration project underway, where the seedlings are propagated within containers in their natural habitat protected by the wild mangrove until large enough to be transplanted.

North of Hainan on the mainland, is Zhanjiang Mangrove NNR on the Leizhou Peninsula, in Guangdong, which together with the Shankou Mangrove NR on eastern Guangxi Zhuang AR coast, lie within the subtropical zone. The dugong (*Dugong dugon*), Chinese white dolphin (*Sousa chinensis chinensis*), horseshoe crab

Left:
Potted mangrove seedlings are cultivated in situ in Dongzhaigang NNR until they are big enough to be planted out in more exposed parts of the coastline.

Below:
Nestling inside an opened cultivated pearl oyster (*Pinctada sp.*) is a pearl, which develops as layers of nacre are laid down around a piece of processed shell introduced inside the mollusc. These bivalves are farmed on Hainan Island.

(*Trachypleus sp.*), pearl oyster (*Pinctada martensii*), black-faced spoonbill and Saunders's gull all occur at Shankou. At low tide, fiddler crabs and mudskippers emerge to feed on the mudflats amongst mangroves.

Mai Po NR is an internationally important wetland reserve on the East Asian Flyway situated on the edge of Deep Bay in Hong Kong. Mangroves, mudflats and traditionally operated shrimp ponds (known locally as *gei wai*) provide food that attracts large numbers of shorebirds during the winter. One *gei wai* is drained every fortnight during the winter from November to March, to provide a rich food source for both migratory shorebirds and winter residents in Deep Bay. Amongst the winter birds which can be seen at Mai Po are Saunders's gull, a quarter of the world's black-faced spoonbills as well as purple herons (*Ardea purpurea*) and Arctic warblers (*Phylloscopus borealis*).

Coral reefs

The distribution of coral reefs worldwide is not determined simply by latitude. For reefs to thrive they require a seawater temperature ranging from 18°C to 30°C. In China, coral growth is mostly limited to tropical Hainan Island, notably along the southern shores, which lie on much the same latitude as Hawaii. Scattered coral colonies do occur on the west coast of Leizhou Peninsula off Guangdong and south of Dongshan Bay off Fujian. They also occur on offshore islands from the north of Taiwan to Weizhou Island and around Hong Kong. If the coastline of mainland China was washed by the warm Kuroshio current, it would extend the northern limit of coral growths.

Large healthy reefs support a rich diversity of reef fishes as well as invertebrate animals. In Hong Kong, Tung Ping Chau and Hoi Ha Wan are marine parks designated specifically to protect coral communities. Hoi Ha Wan has a rich variety of marine life including more than 50 species of coral and 120 species of reef fish. No data is available for fish populations on China's reefs, but both fishermen and divers have noted a marked decline on reefs other than those within the three marine coral reef reserves on mainland China. Typhoons may cause some damage to corals, but in recent years corals have deteriorated as a result of sedimentation, sewage outflow and bomb fishing. The 85 square kilometre Sanya Coral Reef NR in the south of Hainan Island was much damaged in the 1970s and 1980s by local people collecting coral for lime making and as tourist souvenirs. However, the recent upsurge in interest in scuba diving and the popularity of viewing corals through

glass-bottomed boats should now provide an incentive to maintain sustainable reefs, together with the myriad fish, which are associated with healthy reefs.

A future threat to corals reefs worldwide is global warming, for if the sea temperature rises just 1°C above the region's seasonal average for several weeks, coral bleaching can occur and the corals will die. Corals are related to sea anemones; within their limestone skeleton are many polyps that use their tentacles to capture plankton. Within the polyps are algal cells, which convert sunlight into sugars via photosynthesis. It is these sugars which the corals use as their main food source. In return, the algal cells eat the nitrogen waste produced by the coral. Increased seawater temperature blocks the photosynthetic action, so the coral rejects the algae and turns white. If the water cools down and the algae are able to grow again, the coral will recover. Bleaching can also occur as a result of sediments swamping corals and increased exposure to ultra-violet radiation.

Marine mammals and reptiles

Dolphins, whales and seals all occur sparsely in China's coastal waters. The spotted or larga seal (*Phoca largha*) is an Arctic species that occurs around the ice and waters of the North Pacific Ocean and neighbouring seas. These seals migrate through the Sea of Japan, the Yellow Sea and East China Sea to the Spotted Seal NNR at Liaodong Bay, in the Bohai Sea, where sea ice forms on this inland sea in winter. Here the spotted seals come to give birth to their pups on the sea ice in February to March, where they remain until the ice breaks up in March. Seal hunting has been banned since 1983, but with the Chinese population totalling some 1,000 animals, they are regarded as highly endangered in this country. Spotted seals have a varied diet, feeding on crustaceans and cephalopods, as well as several kinds or fish.

Because spotted seals live at the southern edge of the sea ice, their habitat is threatened by climate change. If the ice retreats as a result of global warming, they will be forced to move northwards, where their food resources may be restricted or they may come into more frequent contact with predatory killer whales (orcas).

The Chinese white dolphin is a subspecies of the Indo-Pacific humpback dolphin which appears pink. This colour – unique among dolphins – results from copious surface blood vessels that prevent the body overheating via thermoregulation. Pink dolphins can be seen in Hong Kong waters notably at Sha Chau and Lung Kwu

Above top and centre:
The lion fish (*Pterois sp.*) and the longnose butterfly fish (*Forcipiger flavissimus*) are two of many tropical fish that bring dynamic colour to a healthy coral reef. They are also both popular marine aquarium fish.

Above bottom:
Spotted seals, which occur in China's northern seas, have long sharp claws on their fore flippers which help to grip the ice when moving over floes.

Right:
The green turtle (*Chelonia mydas*) is one of four species of turtles found in Chinese waters. It is so named not from the shell colour but from the flesh inside.

Chau Marine Park. However the dolphins are under threat from heavy boat traffic (engine noise interferes with the dolphins' echo-location), pollution, over-fishing and landfill – the construction of the Chek Lap Kok international airport lost 9.5 square kilometres of dolphin habitat.

Gangkou Turtle NNR in Guangdong is China's smallest reserve covering just eight square kilometres. Green-turtle breeding sites were once widespread in South China, but this is now the sole mainland-nesting beach; all other sites are on offshore islands. Female turtles emerge from the sea at night to laboriously climb up the beach above the high tide level. Here they dig a large hole in which they deposit 100-150 eggs before covering the nest and making their way back to the sea. After 45-70 days incubation, the baby turtle hatchlings emerge and scamper down to the sea to evade predatory gulls. Green turtles as well as leatherback, hawksbill and Ridley turtles all occur in the Yellow Sea. Several species of sea snakes occur in Hong Kong waters as well as off mainland China in the warm, shallow waters of the South China Sea.

Dugongs or sea cows live in warm coastal waters off the southern coast of China, notably around Hainan Island. They are bizarre-looking herbivorous marine mammals that live in wide, but shallow mangrove channels and in shallow protected bays. Here they amble along munching on an almost exclusive diet of sea-grass such as *Halophila ovata* and *Zostera japonica* which, given the right conditions, can form extensive underwater meadows. However, if the sea-grass declines and dugongs fail to get enough food, they will delay their breeding.

Above top:
Predatory orcas or killer whales (*Orcinus orca*) with their dagger-like dorsal fins, move through waters off China's coastline.

Above bottom:
Frosty scallop shells discarded by a processing factory, threaded on ropes ready for seeding with oyster spat on Jiaodong Peninsula in Shandong.

Above:
A sea anemone expands its tentacles in a rock pool ready to grasp a passing prawn or fish.

Below:
Fisherman taking scallop shells on ropes seeded with oyster spat for rearing in deeper water at Jiaodong Peninsula in Shandong.

For centuries, fishermen resisted hunting dugongs because catching one was supposed to bring bad luck. But when new migrants came to Beihai in the 1950s, they had no such qualms about eating dugong meat. It did not take long for local fishermen to discard their superstitions and begin to hunt them as well, with the result that over 200 dugongs were caught from 1957 to 1972.

The Hepu Dugong NNR in Guangxi Zhuang AR helps to protect dugongs and turtles as well as the Chinese white dolphin and mangroves. Elsewhere, within the Gulf of Behai and around Hainan, dugongs are under threat as a result of land reclamation, fish and shrimp pond construction, saltpan farming and agriculture as well as sand, coral and mineral extraction. Until the current status of dugongs in Chinese waters is determined by either aerial or in-depth boat surveys, it will be impossible to appreciate changes in the population.

The diversity of China's coastline is impressive. Nonetheless, pressures from an increasing population and a developing economy threaten these fragile ecosystems and their associated wildlife, as they do throughout the world. A positive development has been the expansion of China's marine reserves. The future of China's natural coastlands depends on the protection of existing reserves, through increased awareness and education within schools and local communities. In addition, where coastal resources are being exploited, alternative livelihood options need to be found, so that future generations can enjoy these unique parts of China's natural heritage.

Appendix

Photographing 'Green China'

Portraying the essence of Green China in just over a year was an ambitious project. Inevitably, some areas could not be covered in the time. Nonetheless examples of all major habitats are included with a selection of their associated wildlife.

This atmospheric dawn shot of the Yuanyang rice terraces in Yunnan involved setting off in complete darkness to arrive on site before it was light. Wearing a head torch I scrambled down a hillside to claim my tripod spot. Only when darkness began to fade did I see the dozens of Chinese photographers assembled around me!

Above:
Using a tripod and flash to photograph a rock pool at Dalian in Liaoning.

Opposite:
A hummingbird hawkmoth (*Macroglossum stellatarum*) makes an obvious humming noise as it hovers to feed on a loofah flower, Xinjiang Uygur AR.

Below right:
Fish are hung up to dry in coastal locations like washing on a line, as here at Dalian.

Even before starting work on this book, I was a veteran traveller to China. My first visit, with a group of New Zealanders' in 1984, was spent exploring mountains in search of wild rhododendrons. Whilst in Wolong, we tried in vain to see the giant pandas, but it was to be another eleven years before I was able to take my first panda pictures.

Getting the images for this book has given me the impetus to visit many new parts of China as well as to revisit some favourite haunts. I travelled to seventeen regions from Harbin at 46°N, to Sanya on Hainan Island at 18°N. Temperatures have ranged from -25°C in Harbin – when my breath froze on the camera, to 35°C in the Turpan Depression. I have worked at elevations from sea level in Shandong and Liaoning, to 4,400 metres in Yunnan searching for choice alpines.

The vast expanse of China makes it impossible to explore more than a few selected locations on any one trip. Once the prime time was known for the key target sites, other side trips could be planned. Without the internet it would have been difficult to research speedily the locations and draw up a provisional itinerary.

Before I leave the UK, my gear has to be packed with military precision. Every item has to be checked off a well-honed equipment list, because I cannot afford to leave behind anything as basic as mains adapters to charge camera batteries, external hard drives and mobile phones. All my leads are packed in colour-coded mesh bags for speedy access.

During each trip I had my own vehicle, driver and English-speaking guide. The drivers rarely speak English, so I soon learnt to call out *'ting ting'* when I wanted to stop. From the onset, the aim was to showcase many of China's stunning landforms and wilderness areas, as well as their associated wildlife. When travelling off the beaten track in China it is essential to expect the unexpected – adverse weather conditions and roads blocked by landslides. The unpredictable nature of wildlife meant that some target objectives failed to materialise; after spending a night in an elevated concrete box I failed to see any Asian elephants in Xishuangbanna; only to discover that the BBC had spent 11 days there before any elephants appeared. On the other hand, unforeseen opportunities constantly arose, with the result that the photo list was always evolving.

Apart from in towns and cities and on expressways, road signs are non-existent in China. Drivers rarely have a road map, so once they are out of their home territory, they don't know the roads. This means repeated stops to ask the way, often resulting

in a complete change of direction, which all takes time; so I try to negotiate an early start to offset expected delays. Yet time was of the essence. To cover the ground in one year, I worked long days with tight schedules. For most of the time I travelled by jeep, but sometimes I had to make do with whatever local transport was available – from bamboo rafts, motorised sampans and high speed boats to horses, cable cars and even a bamboo sedan chair! Wherever possible, I saved time by using a cable car to reach high elevations speedily. I worked from first light to last, often travelling to another location on a night flight, so there would be a mad scramble at the airport to repack the tripod and field clothing in my checked baggage.

Above:
I was thrilled to discover this bizarre cobra lily (*Arisaema elephas*) growing in a forest beside Lake Shuda in Yunnan.

Opposite far left:
Male mandarin duck with reflection of bamboo fence in the Humble Administrator's Garden, Suzhou.

Opposite top:
A simple study of backlit autumn leaves spotted en route to Guilin airport is an example of how less can be more.

Opposite below:
Fingerleaf rodgersia (*Rodgersia aesculifolia*) has superbly textured leaves, Chang Mountain, Dali, Yunnan.

I survived leeches on Hainan, and being bitten by bedbugs at least once in every trip. In remote areas, bedrooms are rarely heated in winter – although it is sometimes possible to scrounge a simple electric bar fire. At two locations it was so cold (0°C) and the bedding so damp, that I had to sleep on top of the bed wearing all my clothes (including my arctic boots)!

At the onset, none of my guides had any clue how I wanted to work. Some were decidedly unenthusiastic about the thought of getting up whilst it was still dark so as to be on site just before dawn, but once we were rewarded with magical first light and I could show them the result on my digital camera, they were just as thrilled as I was. Indeed, most of them soon entered into the spirit of doing their utmost to help me achieve my goals. Many had never been to some of the areas we visited, so it was up to me to discover the best viewpoints at popular tourist spots by buying postcards or, wherever possible, by talking to Chinese photographers who were intrigued to see what gear I used.

While many shots were pre-planned others were quite spontaneous. Like the time we were driving along the seafront in Sanya on Hainan Island, when I spotted an array of water tanks outside a seafood restaurant. Within seconds my driver had done a U-turn and my guide was chatting up the restaurant owner. As the word got round that a strange English lady was photographing shellfish and box crabs in the tanks, one by one the chefs appeared from the kitchen to see me kneeling in sloshing seawater to get the low camera angle I needed.

It is always a gamble deciding where to go when I find I have a few hours to kill in a city before it gets dark. Botanical gardens are very variable in the information they provide, but I usually find something worth taking, even if it is only attractive bark. I entered Urumqi gardens via a minor entrance, where few plants were labelled, but just as I was about to leave I spotted people making a beeline for a marquee. Inside was a display of chrysanthemum flowers of every conceivable colour and shape. Quite by chance I walked out through the back to be greeted by a cloud of butterflies lifting off from a mass of potted chrysanthemums. Never before had I seen such a concentration of butterflies in such a small space.

As well as arranging six long trips during 2007, totalling six months, I also joined two British tour groups – one plant-hunting in Yunnan mountains in summer and the other birding in Zhejiang and Jiangsu in winter. In between trips, I returned to Britain to recharge my own batteries, download all my images and edit them. The main disadvantage of working with digital is the time which has to be spent sitting in front of a computer converting RAW to TIFF image files, adjusting the levels and entering the data in the IPTC fields since our website is designed in such a way it is impossible to upload images unless all the data are complete.

Wherever possible, I used natural light, but for macro work this was sometimes boosted with fill-flash or a reflector. Fill-flash was also used for many animal portraits – notably giant pandas – to gain a highlight in the dark eyes. A tripod was used for most of the images, apart from wildlife action shots. Each evening, all images were backed up by downloading them onto a Jobo Giga Vu Pro 80GB hard drive, which I always carried in my hand baggage.

Amongst the shots I was most pleased to have taken were three that never made the final cut because they did not tie in with the copy. By September, the cotton harvest is in full swing in Xinjiang Uygur AR. When we came across a cotton depot with a cotton 'mountain' towering above the outer walls, I was eager to get some shots.

While my guide, Jimmy, was chatting up the entry guards on the pretext we were interested in exporting cotton, an insect zipped past me towards some yellow loofah flowers and so I slipped inside to check it out. It was a hummingbird hawkmoth, which like its namesake, hovers to feed by rapid wing beats. Without a flash to hand, I had no option but to use a fast shutter speed to freeze the motion of the long tongue probing the flower.

Suzhou has many classical gardens, which I visited in January – not the best time to see the flowering plants – but it is much less crowded than spring or autumn when overseas tours converge on the city. I particularly wanted to revisit some of the gardens to check out the animal and plant designs on the mosaic paths. Within the Humble Administrator's Garden there is a building called the Thirty-six Mandarin Ducks Hall. As we approached, I commented to my guide it was a pity it did not live up to its name by having some mandarin ducks on the adjacent pond; but when we rounded the corner there were the resplendent males together with their rather drab mates. I reached for my long lens to fill the frame, but then spotted a small bamboo fence reflected in the water as fluid abstracts created from the ripples made by the ducks. The lens was swiftly changed for a shorter one so that the ripples became a graphic part of a quintessentially Chinese cameo.

After having seen a poster of Yunnan's Earth Forest in Kunming early in the year, I vowed to visit it in winter when the low angled light would accentuate the surface textures to best advantage. I was not disappointed. The dramatic landforms were offset against a clear blue sky – the reason why Yunnan is much favoured by filmmakers because it is remote from the aerial pollution emanating from many Chinese cities.

In researching this book I discovered locations where the prime time to visit coincided with another far flung part of China, therefore one had to be sacrificed for the other. Nonetheless, I shall return to seek out and record more facets of the natural world within this fascinating and fast-developing country, so I have an even broader picture of Green China as I saw it in the early part of the twenty-first century.

Opposite above:
Painted lady butterflies (*Vanessa cardui*) feed on potted chrysanthemums in Urumqi Botanic Garden.

Opposite below:
A fun shot spotted after emerging from a tropical butterfly house: feeding tracks of a slug or snail have rasped the algal film inside the glass.

Right:
One of my favourite giant panda pictures – showing a youngster surveying the winter forest from the fork of a tree.

Cameras and lenses

Nikon D2X digital cameras
Nikon AF-S Nikkor 12-24mm f4 G ED
  zoom lens
Nikon AF-S Nikkor 24-120mm lens f3.5/5.6 G
  zoom lens
Nikon AF-S VR105mm f2.8 G Micro-Nikkor lens
Nikon AF 70-180mm f4.5-5.6 Micro-Nikkor
  zoom lens
Nikon AF VR Nikkor 80-400mm f4.5-5.6 D
  zoom lens
Nikon AF-S Nikkor f4 G 200-400mm zoom lens
Nikon AF-S Nikkor f4 D 500mm lens

Other equipment

SanDisc Extreme IV 4GB CF cards
Nikon SB-800 speedlight
Stofen flash diffuser
Visible Dust Arctic Butterfly sensor brush
Jobo Giga Vu Pro 80GB hard drive
Gitzo GT3540 Carbon 6X tripod
Gitzo G1475M ball head
Benbo tripod for working in water –
  caves and rocky shores
Really Right Stuff BH-55 ball head
Beanbag
Lastolite reflectors and diffusers
Cameramac waterproof cover
Umbrella to protect camera
Tripod leg warmers
Chemical hand warmers
Field notebook – packed with contacts,
  scientific names, and quotes from local
  people and naturalists

Bibliography

Angel, Heather, *Panda*, David and Charles (2008)

Caidan, An, *Travel Guide to Tibet of China*, China Intercontinental Press (2003)

Chinese National Geography, *Scenic Splendor of China*, Beijing: New Star Press (2006)

Cizu, Zhang, *China: Rare Wild Animals*, Beijing: Foreign Languages Press (2002)

Corrigan, Gina, *Odyssey Illustrated Guide to Guizhou*, Hong Kong: Guidebook Company Ltd (1995)

Ji, Zhao et al. *The Nature History of China*, London: William Collins & Sons and Co Ltd (1990)

Kaiyong, Lang, et al. *Alpine Flowering Plants in China*, Beijing: China Esperanto Press (1997)

Keswick, Maggie, *The Chinese Garden: History, Art and Architecture*, London: Academy Editions and New York: St. Martin's Press (1986) 2nd Edition.

Lancaster, Roy, *Roy Lancaster Travels in China: A Plantman's Paradise*, Woodbridge, Suffolk, UK: Antique Collectors' Club Ltd (1989)

Lau, Theodora, *The Handbook of Chinese Horoscopes*, London: Arrow Books (1981)

MacKinnon, John and Phillipps, Karen, *A Field Guide to the Birds of China*, New York: Oxford University Press (2000)

Matthiessen, Peter, *The Birds of Heaven: Travels with Cranes*, London: Vintage (2003)

Quanan, Wu, *Wild Flowers of Yunnan in China*, Beijing: China Forestry Publishing House (1999)

Schaller, George B., *The Last Panda*, Chicago and London: University of Chicago Press (1993)

Sivin, Prof Nathan, et al. *The Contemporary Atlas of China*, London: Weidenfeld and Nicolson (1988)

State Council Information Office of China, *World Heritage Sites in China*, China Intercontinental Press (2003)

Temple, Robert K.G., *China: Land of Discovery and Invention*, UK: Patrick Stephens Limited (1986)

Vainker, Shelagh, *Chinese Silk: A Cultural History*, New Brunswick, New Jersey: Rutgers University Press (2004)

Valder, Peter, *The Garden Plants of China*, London: Weidenfeld and Nicolson, and Florilegium: Balmain, NSW, Australia (1999)

Williams, C.A.S., *Chinese Symbolism and Art Motifs*, Tokyo, Singapore and Vermont: Tuttle Publishing (2006) 4th Edition

Wilson, E.H., *A Naturalist in Western China*, London: Cadogan Books Ltd (1986)

Wiltshire, Trea, *Bamboo*, Hong Kong: FormAsia Books Ltd (2004)

Winchester, Simon, *The River at the Centre of the World: a Journey up the Yangtze, and Back in Chinese Time*, London: Penguin Books (1996)

Xiyang, Tang, *Living Treasures: An Odyssey Through China's Extraordinary Nature Reserves*, Beijing: Bantam Press (1988)

Yarong, Wang, *Chinese Folk Embroidery*, London: Thames and Hudson (1987)

Ying, Wong Kang and Dahlen, Marta, *Streetwise Guide Chinese Herbal medicine*, San Francisco: Red Mansions (2000)

Yin, Yang, *The Charms of China*, China Nationality Art Photograph Publishing House (2006)

Zhongmin, Lu, *China: Folk Handicrafts*, Beijing: Foreign Languages Press (2002)

Index of Scientific Names

Index